PERSPECTIVES ON ASCENSION

Sustenance for Humanity's Journey Home

Dawn Fleming

A compilation of joy and wisdom

Infinite Wisdom Press, a division of
Energy Transformations, Inc.
1700 E. Butler Circle
Chandler, AZ 85225
U.S.A.

reikidawn@yahoo.com
http://www.energytransformations.org

Copyright © 2008 Infinite Wisdom Press. All rights reserved. No part of this booklet may be reproduced or transmitted in any form or by any means, electronic or mechanical, including photocopying, recording, or emailing, or by any information storage and retrieval system, without written permission from the author, except for the inclusion of brief quotations in a review.

ISBN 978-0-6152-3930-9

Book Created and Presented by
Dawn Fleming

Editors
Toni Neal and Dawn Fleming

Cover Image – Inner Light
by Paul Heussenstamm
www.mandalas.com

Cover Design
Amanda Sachs and Dawn Fleming

Technical Assistance
Amanda Sachs

This book is dedicated to all of the people seeking enlightenment who are working on their individual healing processes to assist our earth's and humanity's ascension into a place of peace – creating heaven on earth.

Many thanks to all those who made this book possible with your contributions, prayers, and enthusiasm. Big thanks to Bill, my husband, who cheers me on and offers great technical assistance. Much gratitude to all the hard work and encouragement from Amanda Sachs and Toni Neal.

Dawn Fleming

CONTENTS

Introduction		5
Poem	Who You Are	9
Chapter 1	Ascension 101	11
Chapter 2	Joy, Gratitude, and Light	23
Poem	Present With What Is	33
Chapter 3	Living in the Core	35
Chapter 4	Preparing the Body to Receive and Maintain Ascension Energy	51
Poem	Every Step Is Holy	69
Chapter 5	Answering the Call	71
Chapter 6	Living Space to Sacred Space Creating Transcendent Environments	83
Poem	On the Other Side	103
Chapter 7	A Funny Thing Happened on the Way to Ascension	105
Chapter 8	AWAKE – A Sufi Ascension Practice	121
Poem	Let it Go	137
Chapter 9	Releasing Attachments	139
Chapter 10	The Twelve Steps on the Stairway to Heaven: The Path Up and Out from Food Addiction	147
Poem	Be the Energy	163
Chapter 11	Ascension: Life at the Peaks	165
Chapter 12	The Path of Ascension	191
Bibliography and Footnotes		209

Introduction

The idea for *Perspectives on Ascension* came to me after a presentation on Harnessing the Higher Energies, my first mini-conference that I organized and presented in July 2007. Spirit then downloaded the ideas and direction of this amazing book. Up to this point my writing projects, i.e. books, articles and manuals, were solo endeavors. Even though I was and still am working on my own book about ascension, I was instructed to invite other enlightened writers to contribute chapters to this book.

Ascension is a word that has many meanings depending on where you are in life. To get all of the writers in synch with Spirit's vision for this book, I provided my own views on ascension and what I wanted *Perspectives on Ascension* to embody.

Ascension – to rise above our problems and fears; to move into a higher state of consciousness; to lift us into the Higher Self or God consciousness that knows and lives from a place of Oneness with the Beloved. When we embody ascension consciousness we know our infinite nature and realize the many possible expressions of the Divine. We bring forth the Divine into all areas of our lives.

Ascension is also transcending from the limited self-expression of the ego into the infinite expression of the Higher Self. When we are aligned with the Higher Self, we do not worry about the world's perceptions of how we live our life.

On another level, ascension occurs when we raise our energetic vibration through meditation, prayer, mindful living and being present. We move into the cosmic consciousness aware of the Ascended Beings and their connection with humanity. In this sphere of ascension, we work with these Ascended Masters to bring forth God's Plan of Love, Perfection, Truth, and Wisdom for the entire planet.

Is ascending our ego in this life possible? Can we ascend into the realms of cosmic consciousness? Yes, all this is possible and more! By embarking on this ascension sojourn, we delve into our inner world to heal, transform and raise our consciousness to support quintessential life changes, freeing ourselves and humanity to create Heaven on earth. The Ascended Masters are supporting us to enter more deeply into knowing our authentic selves. Their loving energy along with our own personal quest for our connection with the Divine are making ascension possible for each of us in this lifetime as we become masters of our mind, body, emotions, and spirit.

Although I try to define this arcane concept, ascension defines itself within us as we experience the process and realize the immeasurable energy and grace that unfolds along the way. Relating the words of Lao Tzu in the Tao Te Ching to defining ascension, to name it is to elude its essence. So let us move out of defining ascension into observing how ascension impacts us as individuals and as a human race and derive our own meaning from our personal experiences.

The writers in Perspectives on Ascension provide sustenance to guide and to feed us as we engage these new realms within and around us. They remind us of the ancient teachings and bring new perspectives on how to embrace the initiations that come with this unchartered territory. They speak to the ups and downs in our exploration, and how we can prepare our body, mind and spirit to support ascension. In-depth information is provided on creating transcendent environments, releasing attachments, addressing addictions, and working with the Ascended Masters. In this book the writers provide instruction, techniques and ideas to delve into to master this transformational process. The gifts of joy, gratitude, humor and love are extended to us as we take in the perspectives that the writers offer. We are asked to move into our Core and to practice Radical Self Care[©].

The beautiful poetry of Danna Faulds speaks to our hearts and bids us to move out of our comfort zones, to be fully present, and to trust the flow of life. Her poetry provides inspiration as we move into the unknown into the core of our Presence.

Savor the words in this book. Know that we are not alone in our quest to evolve and to seek the freedom to be who we were birthed to be – ascended and free.

In Peace,
    In Love,
        In Grace,
            Dawn Fleming

Who You Are

Who you are is so much more
than what you do. The essence,
shining through heart, soul, and
center, the bare and bold truth
of you does not lie in your
to-do list. You are not just
at the surface of your skin, not
just the impulse to arrange the
muscles of your face into a smile
or a frown, not just boundless
energy, or bone wearying fatigue.
Delve deeper. You are divinity;
the vast and open sky of Spirit.
It is the light of God, the ember
at your core, the passion and the
presence, the timeless, deathless
essence of you that reaches out
and touches me. Who you are
transcends fear and turns
suffering into liberation;
Who you are is love.

    Danna Faulds, from her book *Go In and In*

CHAPTER 1

Ascension 101

Elizabeth Spear

How many times have you asked yourself: "Why am I here?" or "What is my purpose, my reason for being?" or "What are my life's lessons?" Perhaps you have felt a longing to "go home," not even knowing where that real Home may be. Yes, we have our Earthly parents and our Heavenly parents, our Father-Mother God.

These questions began for me when I was a young adult. They led me to the Edgar Cayce materials, and from there, to the study of Yoga. Forty years later, I am still a serious Yoga Chela. I was greatly blessed in those early years by some special teachers, including Paramahansa Yogananda, author of *Autobiography of a Yogi*. From Yogananda, I was led to Kriya Yoga disciplines and teachings. The higher realisms began to surface for me with the incredible Ascended

Masters' books and teachings, such as *Unveiled Mysteries* and *The Magic Presence* by Guy Ballard (whose Ascended name is Godfree Ray King). Saint Germain's Love for All Humanity and His awesome ascension teachings really spoke to my heart and soul as being Divine Truths.

I have always known that we are all Sons and Daughters of a Most High, Living God; a God of Unconditional, Divine Love for all Life, everywhere. I began to understand that our home, planet Earth, is a schoolroom, where we learn how to be *in* the world, but not *of* it. We came here to learn how to be God in Action, here and now, as God needs our bodies. We are all made in God's image, and each of us has a drop of that Divine Essence. Sometimes I think of us as separate drops of water. But when we all come together, we become a beautiful ocean in Unity Consciousness. We are One; we are Unity; I am you, and you are me. So in reality, our mission is to co-create Heaven on Earth.

Our quantum physicists tell us that everything is energy, vibration and consciousness, vibrating at different rates or ratios of speeds. Once upon a time, a very long time ago, our planet was vibrating at a very high state of consciousness. Earth was moving along very well; so well, that the Confederation of Planets decided that it would be helpful to bring some laggard souls here to Earth, where they could benefit and grow in our high state of evolution. These laggard souls were holding back evolution on their own home planet, and it was felt that by incarnating here on Earth, they would be brought up to our then - higher state of evolutionary consciousness. The experimental plan did not work because of the negative and dark forces. It ended in cataclysms, chaos and upheavals due to the Universal law of cause and effect (Karma). The continent of Lemuria in the Pacific Ocean sank with sixty million souls.

This time, however, it is going to be different. The ancient yogic text describes a Yuga, which roughly occurs every 24,000 years, where everything in the universe is moved up the Spiral of Evolution into the next higher octave of Universal Consciousness. Our planet Earth is at a critical turning point and it is graduation time in God's Schoolroom. The Yuga time is now and our consciousness is being urged to go with the flow and expand into higher frequencies of energy, vibration, and consciousness.

We are being told from the Higher Realms that this planet and all her life will be ascending into the fourth dimension, and then, by our God Parents' Grace, it will move very rapidly into the fifth dimension, which is more harmonious. Actually, we will move into a glorious, promised Golden Age of life without aging, where all enjoy optimal health, unlimited prosperity and abundance. If one understands music, it can be understood as moving up into a higher octave where Peace, Prosperity, Divine Love and Light reign supreme.

The Beloved Saint Germain has been working with all of humanity for a very long time, preparing us to ascend. In *The Magic*

Presence, Saint Germain channels information to Godfree Ray King about an Ascension Chair that he created. This chair exists in the etheric realms of our planet, and we may call on Saint Germain and ask to be taken to it, beyond sleep. If we can live in our Hearts of Unconditional Divine Love, as Saint Germain and other Ascended Masters teach, we can ascend on our own.

The Ascended Masters are just that - our Higher Brothers and Sisters who so lovingly teach us how to be God in Action, here and now, with every breath we take. Are we qualifying each breath with love, trust, truth, peace, harmony, balance, and all the finer qualities? Or, are we miscreating with negative energies of anger, frustration and the rest of the lower energies? It is our free-will choice.

This is our lesson and our reason for being. Only when we are vibrating at these very high frequencies all the time will we be allowed to ascend. It is all a matter of energy and vibration, and we do it ourselves, with our consciousness. Our time is at hand and we can do this with correct, free-will choices. The Ascended Masters and the Angelic kingdom are here to offer us all the assistance we need, but because we live on a planet of free will, we have to ask for their assistance. Then, by Cosmic Law, they are so ready to help us. They cannot do it for us, but upon asking, we will immediately receive their help and guidance. We each must earn our Ascension, and this time, it will be permanent.

The Ascended Masters teach how to connect consciously with our mighty I AM presence, our highest God Selves, and move into Christ Consciousness, having Unconditional, Divine Love for all Life, everywhere. We can ask, affirm, and bring this Highest Self energy down through our crown chakra and through our bodies with every breath we take. We can invoke this Divine Essence to flow though us daily, hourly, always before meditation, and especially prior to doing healings.

About fifteen years ago, I was blessed by being introduced to Drunvalo Melchizedek and his teachings of the Sacred Geometries of the Flower of Life and Merkaba Meditation. Drunvalo gave us profound information on Ascension. He said every one of us can access Christ Consciousness just by practicing the Merkaba Breath Meditation. The word Merkaba is three words: mer is light, ka is spirit, and ba is the physical body. The Merkaba technology is mastering counter-rotating fields of energy. Our DNA molecule is an example of a counter-rotating field vortex of Merkaba energy. Drunvalo claims that we already know what he is teaching; he is just helping us remember who we are and why we are here.

The Flower of Life information is already within us. Just by focusing our attention on the beautiful Flower of Life Mandala, we begin to unlock codes of energy, the ancient teachings of the Seed of Life, and knowledge of the Tree of Life, along with the Sacred Geometry of the Platonic Solids information. This begins our remembrance of our Ascension and homeward journey.

Flower of Life Mandala

This Flower of Life Symbol Mandala has appeared all over the world, including ancient carvings on pyramid walls. There was even an ancient three dimensional form found in the Orient. And in 1955, a crop circle of the Flower of Life appeared in Northern England.

Dunvalo eloquently explains the difference between the normal death process, Resurrection, and Ascension. When a person goes through the death process (or the physical body dies), they go immediately into the Void state, and then into the third overtone of the fourth dimension. A dimension is a waveform energy of a sine wave. Sine waves correspond to light and the vibration of sound. Overtones refer to octaves, as in music. When one is in the third overtone of the fourth dimension, they are unconscious, retaining no memory of either the death process or the other side of the veil, and have no control over the image. They are therefore unable to use the Merkaba field and will cycle back into Earth's existence over and over, or what we call reincarnation. When you reincarnate back into Earth in another physical body, you have no memory of where you have come from, either. Reincarnation has been a slow process; a revolving door that has kept us going without memory for a very long time. Thus, the lessons we came to learn from this process have been extremely slow indeed.

With the knowledge of the Merkaba energy field and how to use our Living Light Vehicle, one is able to move through with memory intact, and thus have immortality. Drunvalo defines Resurrection as going through the death of the physical body with memory intact, using the Merkaba. After one dies, the physical body is dropped, and then through memory, one recreates the Light body and goes through a process that leads them into the tenth, eleventh or twelfth overtone of the fourth dimension. From there, there is no more reincarnation. One continues into Eternal Life and memory is no longer blocked.

There is a far greater difference in Ascension. In Ascension there is no death process as we know it. One is no longer on Earth, but their physical body did not die. It became pure Light through the use of the Merkaba teaching (whether one remembered it, or one was taught it). One passes through the Void totally conscious, going on to the higher dimensions, aware of the whole process. Whereas the normal death process involves the reconstructing of another human body (reincarnation), and in Resurrection, a Light body, in Ascension, one simply walks out by disappearing from this dimension and reappearing in the next (after passing through the void).

With the completion of the Ascension grid for this planet by the Realms of Illumined Truths in 1989, our planet can now ascend. Prior to that time, ascension was highly unlikely. There were some exceptions; those who were highly enough evolved in consciousness to make their Ascension into the Light and became Holy, Ascended and Free.

By using the knowledge of our Merkaba, or our Living Light Vehicle, Ascension is now completely possible. Some people will still die and go through the normal death process, going to the third overtone and into a holding pattern for a while. But, as previously mentioned, our planet, Mother Earth, is also in an Ascension process, as are all the planets in our Universe. All are destined to move up an octave in energy, vibration, and consciousness. When these changes come, all people who were holding on that third overtone will also rise up to the same dimensional level as those who resurrected or ascended. In the Bible, it states that the dead will rise up. Just as water exists in three states -liquid (water), gas (steam), or solid (ice), there are different states of being - but really no such thing as death.

Drunvalo and the Ascended Masters tell us that the time for reincarnation is now over (there are always exceptions to the rule); but this is our last lifetime in a three-dimensional body, and only God knows how long it will be until we ascend. It all has to do with vibration, consciousness and energy.

As we increase our love and wisdom, meaning Unconditional Divine Love for all Life everywhere, we then, through wisdom, are able to give love wisely and receive love wisely given. The secret key is to be living in our heart center of compassion without judgments. We are being asked every moment of this life to live wisely with the four forms of energy we have been given: thoughts, words, actions and feeling.

To state it simply-are we actually loving all life, completely and totally, with every thought we think, every word we say, every action we take, and every feeling we have towards another? For example: Is there perhaps a neighbor down the street that we can honestly say we love unconditionally (without any judgments), no matter how they are behaving? This is what we are being asked to do; to give up all judgments and live in our Hearts of Compassion, having Love for all Life, everywhere.

Are we going to pass this final initiation? It is totally up to each one of us; no one else can do it for us.

May there be love, trust, peace, truth, harmony, beauty and balance throughout the Cosmos; and may your remembrance of the Merkaba be a blessing unto you. All is well; God Loves You; and so do I.

About Elizabeth Spear

Elizabeth Spear is a Registered Nurse, a certified Psychiatric/Mental Health Nurse, and holds a Master Degree in Psychology. For many years she worked in traditional medicine and has spent her adult life honing and perfecting both traditional and alternative healing skills. She is a certified Hypnotherapist, and is also certified in Eye Movement Desensitization Therapy. Elizabeth increases her skills with new modalities as Spirit directs. As a result she is also certified to teach the following complimentary pathways:

- Joyful Child Parenting class facilitator, fostering Spiritual Growth in Children of all ages.
- Theta Healing (DNA) Facilitator-DNA activation techniques as received and taught by Vianna Stibel.
- Flower of Life/Sacred Geometry/Merkaba Meditation Facilitator. Elizabeth was trained by Drunvalo Melchizedek in 1995 and has been facilitating this workshop all over the country for 13 years.
- Yoga Instructor for 40 years, having had numerous yoga instructors both in the USA and abroad.

Elizabeth is pleased to develop a Flower of Life/ Merkaba Workshop in your area for you and your friends.

Visit www.elizabethspear.com for lists of classes and contact information.

CHAPTER 2

Joy, Gratitude, and Light

Bob Tucker

I'm going to tell you, right up front, why it is extremely important to allow yourself to feel more joy and gratitude. Telling you up front serves two purposes: I make sure that you get the kernel of information that I want to pass along; and you don't have to be bored silly reading the esoteric maundering of someone you don't know. After all, some of you are already experienced seekers and are probably familiar with what I have to say about healing and energy work.

So here it is:

By allowing yourself to experience more joy and gratitude, you are opening up a channel for greater Light and healing to enter into your life. That's it! Pretty simple, right? Feel more joy and gratitude; receive more Light and healing. So now you know what I wanted to tell you, and you can go on and read the more interesting parts of this book. Enjoy!

Wait! What's that comment? It's easy for me to say, "Feel more joy and gratitude"? But I don't know anything about your life, or the challenges you face, so how can I ask you to feel more joy and gratitude? Well, before I answer, let me tell you a little about my own life.

I was a law enforcement officer for thirty years. You see a lot of things in three decades of being a cop, things that at times tend to take a serious toll on your opinion of humanity. After I retired from law enforcement, I ran my own business as a private contractor with the U.S. Department of Defense for a few years. I gave that up when I received a diagnosis of kidney cancer, followed shortly thereafter by the unexpected death of my mother. So I know something about human emotions and the dark side of things, both from observation and direct experience.

Nothing is ever the same after a cancer diagnosis. The world that seemed so solid and predictable before, now suddenly seemed full of uncertainty. Although the surgery was a success, and my doctor confirmed that I had recovered physically from the operation, mentally and emotionally I felt devastated. Life seemed to have lost most of its meaning. I tried hard to rise above this devastated feeling, but I found it very difficult to do. Fear filled my life; almost anything could send me into a panic and depression. My doctor could only offer pills and more tests, and I was not willing to live a life filled with constantly more invasive testing and prescription drugs.

Just when I was beginning to feel that I could no longer cope, an old friend suggested that I try something called Reiki. Isn't it strange how, sometimes, a seemingly terrible disaster leads to an unexpected and perfectly wonderful treasure? There are times when we just have to trust a Higher wisdom to guide us. That first Reiki treatment changed my life just as profoundly as had the cancer, but in an entirely different way. I felt as though the Reiki Master had pulled back a curtain in a dark room, and the sun shone in to chase away the darkness. I knew at that moment that I wanted to learn all about this healing method. I wanted to become a Reiki healer.

I've accomplished that goal by becoming a Usui and Lightarian Reiki Master, which was an amazing journey in itself. But that is another story. Life's journey often leads us to unexpected places, and we experience important lessons along the way. We tend to fit these lessons into the categories of good, bad, or neutral experiences. When we think about gratitude, we usually relate it to the "good" experiences because that's what we have always been taught. Good things mean God loves us; bad things mean God is unhappy with us. Most of us, by that definition, can find something to be grateful for: love, family, good health, a house, and a job that helps us have all that we think we want. Even the poorest among us can find something to be thankful for, like a warm meal from a soup kitchen, a handout from a generous passerby, or a place to stay on a cold night. But the painful experiences can be the source of some of our greatest life lessons. I did not give you that little capsule history of my life to garner sympathy, but to show you that I have a few of my own scars. I believe that life is an adventure full of experiences that we have carefully chosen, including the "bad" ones, and we need to learn to be grateful for all of them.

So how do we learn to bring more joy and gratitude into our life? Well, I didn't say that this would be easy, at least not in the beginning. It's not really difficult either, but as with all inner work, it requires a certain amount of persistence. The more you practice, the more grateful you will become, and the more joy you will feel. You may even notice a cascade effect. But you have to do the work. Just reading about it is not enough. You might start by asking yourself what are some of the things that bring you joy.

My wife and children are sources of my joy. But we don't always have to look for the big things to find it. As adults we sometimes forget about the small things that used to bring us joy as children: smelling fresh cut grass, watching a storm coming, the scent of rain in the air on a hot day, the smell of honeysuckle blossoms in the summer, or walking in the falling snow in the winter. These are some of the little things that still bring me joy today. Try looking back at some of the things that made you happy before you allowed yourself to be locked into your adult life. You may be surprised at how the memory will return some of that joy to you, and how grateful you will feel.

Another tool that we can use to bring more joy and gratitude into our life is the practice of meditation. Meditation in the traditional sense has always been difficult for me, as my mind tends to wander and a thousand things want to intrude. I have found that using Reiki symbols, music, guided meditation, and sitting outside with nature, all tend to help me reach that calm place inside where I can get in touch with the Source of life's blessings.

But you don't have to do any formal meditation to start your journey to feeling more gratitude and joy. You can start simply by counting your blessings. That's really all. You can do this at bedtime, (remember the old saying "Count your blessings instead of sheep"?), or you can do this at anytime during the day when you can afford a moment.

Start by thinking of a blessing in your life, any blessing. Try seeing that blessing as a seed, a living diamond, brilliant with potential. See yourself planting that seed into your heart, and imagine it growing into a beautiful flower. I like to imagine a beautiful red rose. Watch the flower open, and feel all the joy, happiness, and wonder of life bursting forth from the center of the opening flower. Repeat to yourself, or say out loud, "I am grateful," three times. Hold on to this feeling as long as you can.

Practice this as often as you can in a day. It does not take long and it is not complicated. In between, think about what is good in your life -- anything at all, even seemingly small things. Maybe the coffee or tea tastes particularly good today; maybe the traffic is not as bad as usual, or perhaps you found a good parking space. You can find something if you look.

Make it a habit to find something to be grateful for each day. The more you look, the more you will find. And at least once a day, plant that seed of blessing into your heart. If you wish, you can be more formal with it as a practice. Light a candle; place your hands together in prayer position at the level of your heart; do some centered breathing; listen to music; or try any other techniques that help you relax and visualize. The important thing is to allow yourself to feel the joy and gratitude grow within you, and acknowledge it.

We all have days when the world seems to be too much to handle. It's easy to forget that we are actually spiritual beings; that we are only here in the physical for a short while. Find that spot in your heart where you can grow the seed of gratitude and joy. Plant that seed and nurture it; then you will have an edge. You will have a place to look for Light when things seem dark. The more you practice, the easier it will be to find that place when you need it. As it becomes easier for you, you will begin to look differently at everything in your life. You may start to see all your life experiences in a positive way, even those that you used to judge as "bad." Just open yourself to that possibility.

When you can really begin to feel grateful for every experience in your life, you will discover other benefits, such as having less anger. With less anger in your life there is automatically more room for joy and happiness. Joy and happiness in a person's life promotes good health, and generosity and kindness toward others. Generosity and kindness toward others will return to you many times over creating even more for which to be grateful.

See what I mean about a cascade effect? You may even find a calm surfacing that you did not have before in your life. When you are able to hold on to that calm for a while, it may be easier to feel the living Light that resides within you.

Gautama Buddha is said to have told his disciples that we are made of Light. The Old Testament says that God's first words were, "Let there be Light." We are a part of that Light. We come from the Light, and it is our destiny to return to the Light. Even in our physical body Light always surrounds us and connects us. Living brilliant Light, rainbows of Light, magnificent, wonderful Light! We are never truly in the dark; it's just that most of us cannot see the Light because we have shut out everything but the physical world. But you can learn to sense, to "feel" the Light, to know that it is there without physically seeing it, once you have opened yourself to those feelings of gratitude, joy, and happiness and released some anger. Those qualities will untie some of the knots that keep you bound so tightly into the stresses and fears of the physical world, making room for more Light to manifest.

As you become more Light-filled, you not only experience the positive effects, you have a positive effect on those that you come in contact with because you carry that Light wherever you go. Whether you realize it or not, you interact at a higher, unseen level with others all the time. Whenever you come into contact with others, your energies meet. When you carry higher levels of Light, you may notice that people tend to smile at you more and seek your company. Surprising things can happen in ordinary circumstances when you allow your Light to shine. Adults will often notice a positive change in you they cannot define, and children in particular seem to be able to sense those who radiate more Light.

After you have been practicing for a while life begins to seem less difficult and arbitrary. This is because even if your outer world appears unchanged, your inner world is becoming far more beautiful. You are beginning to live at a higher vibration. You will find that while others still complain about the darkness, you can see things differently because you have lit a candle against the dark. And when you send joy, gratitude and Light out into the world, you are sending healing as well.

No matter where you are or who you are on this planet, you are connected by the Web of Life. You can never truly be separated from your Source. You are truly loved, and always surrounded by those that want to help and guide you. Your Core Being is bright with Light and Energy, and can never really lose its way, no matter how your physical body may perceive things. Your Core Being remains radiant, beautiful, and unharmed. The more deeply you understand that connection, the more you want to preserve the world that you live in.

Practicing joy and gratitude can open doors for you that you might not be able to fully access any other way. It leads you to the mountaintop. The Light that already resides within you will serve to illuminate a world far greater than you realize exists.

I honor the Light that is within you! I hope you find joy and a sincere depth of gratitude every day. I hope the seed of joy and gratitude that you plant in your heart blooms into a magnificent flower that radiates happiness and Light for you and everyone around you!

Namaste!

About Bob Tucker

Bob Tucker is a Usui and Lightarian Reiki Master, with all six Lightarian Rays. He spent three decades as a law enforcement officer, before retiring to run his own business as a government contractor. He is a kidney cancer survivor, married, and the father of three children. Bob is currently a Reiki practitioner and can be contacted at:

Kelly's Herb House and Wellness Center

401 Headquarters Drive

Millersville, Maryland 21108

Present With What Is

Even as I rest my attention
on the unwavering center,
I see that nothing stays the
same. The moment is
dynamic, changing.
When I try to frame it,
freeze it, pin it down
I lose the fluidity of now.

My urge to grow nudges me
beyond my comfort zone.
In order to evolve, I enter
the unknown and become
mobile, mutable, versatile.

Evolution and perfection
coincide, inviting me to
expand my view until I
see two as one, and one
as the sum of every change
and circumstance. I savor
this gift of living fully
present with what is.

Danna Faulds, *Prayers to the Infinite*

CHAPTER 3

Living in the Core

Kimberly James

As incarnated souls, we have the blessing of a vast home in which to live – a home that can be divided into many rooms. We have the room of our mind, where our thoughts and ideas flow freely. In the room of our body, our bones, organs, and cells are sourced and provide the sensory information we need to exist on this plane. There is the room of our emotions, where our experiences are organized into the ebb and flow of feelings, rising and falling within us. And finally, the room of our spirit houses our connection to source and to all other beings. Our heart, where compassion and love reign, can integrate all of these rooms into a home.

Each room offers individual blessings and gifts, as each is a sacred piece of the puzzle of ourselves. In this chapter, you will explore your relationship to each room, and learn how to transition beyond these rooms into the space of your Core.

The Core is the essential essence inherent in all of us, which we experience as a continuum along the plane of existence. As you journey along your path to ascension, it is through living in the Core that you will find your individual experience of the divine that lies within.

I am aware of my thoughts. I am more than just my mind.

Awareness seeks a space in your home. It is the mind consciousness, or the mental body, that grants us the opportunity to gain a deeper knowledge and understanding of ourselves and the world. The mind is the temple of thoughts, perceptions, and illusions. This room, in the home of your soul, is the center of discernment and judgment. The mind consciousness says, "I think therefore I am."

Let's visualize this room. Take a few moments to get centered, by taking a few slow, deep breaths. Close your eyes, and visualize yourself in front of a doorway. This doorway is the entry point to the mind's room in your home. Notice its dimensions, color, texture, thickness, and translucence. Is the doorway welcoming or foreboding? Does it have signage announcing that it is the room of the mind, or is it unmarked, its depths unplumbed and mysterious?

How do you feel standing in front of it? Are you comforted by its presence? Is it a place you visit frequently? What do you hear as you stand at the doorway? What do you smell, taste, touch, and sense about this place?

Take a moment to relax into the space of this doorway, and when you're ready, open your eyes and record your experience. As you review your experience of this entryway, note anything that surprised you. Did something unexpected occur?

Our mental body is a very powerful consciousness. As we journey along the path, the awareness formed by the mental body about who we are, who we are not, and who we are in relation to the world is a fundamental source of introspection and healing. We explore the story of our childhood, parents, spouse, job, and beyond through the mind. We are able to develop an understanding of our stimulus and response patterns, while taking responsibility for our actions. We can live with mindfulness, observing ourselves through the lens of the mental eye. It is through our mind that so much of our identity is formed, deconstructed, and then reformed.

Through this consciousness, we are able to use our thoughts to co-create reality. As we examine our thoughts, perceptions, and judgments, the mental body allies with us to reframe our experiences from negative to positive, chaotic to ordered, and inconsequential to destined. This mind energy gives us the power to rewrite stories of victimization into tales of heroism.

Take a moment to return to the doorway of your mind consciousness. Inhale deeply and slowly, and when you are ready, enter the room. Allow all your senses to expand. What do you smell, taste, touch, hear, and see? Allow the mind to rest quietly as you observe only with your senses this room.

What are the room's dimensions? How high is the ceiling, if one exists? Where are you in the room—the center, entry, or corner? What is in front of you, to the sides of you, and behind you? Is there anyone else in the room with you? Is this room well lived in? Is this room furnished, and if so, how? Does the room change as you move through it? Explore it as thoroughly as you can.

Find a space in the room that feels safe and comfortable. Relax into this space and ask, "What message does this room want to share with me right now?" Be open to the experience of receiving a word, a sentence, or an image. A piece of paper may appear, or a song may play. In any form that arises, allow the room to express itself fully to you. After experiencing all that the room has to offer, return to the doorway and offer gratitude to this room for its gifts.

When you are ready, open your eyes and record your experiences. What was surprising about this room? Were you able to experience the room with just your senses, without judgment? How does the message this room provided resonate with you?

I am present in my body. I am more than just my body.

The body is the vessel that houses our experiences and our lives. The body is a complex consciousness, with systems layered upon systems, all of which are innately wise. The DNA and cells have both purpose and programming, the bones create structure and harmonize our form, the organs allow a balance between internal and external, and we experience the flow of fluids and states of being in each moment of the day. Events are encoded in the body consciousness in a way that is not accessible to the mind. It embodies our experiences in a truth that is not overshadowed by judgment—it just is. The body consciousness says, "I have form, therefore, I am."

Using the same steps described above, connect to the doorway to the room of the body. Record your experience of this entryway, objectively identifying anything that was surprising or unexpected. Try to release any judgment you may have about the experience.

The body is our ally as we determine how we want to formulate our beingness on this plane. We inherit our characteristics from genealogy, childhood, and karmic connections. They all come into the body ready for integration and healing. Our bodies tell our stories without words. The scar on a knee, the residual pain from an accident, the resulting dis-ease from an event that may have occurred half a lifetime ago—these are all within the body consciousness.

As we explore the encoding and programming that exist within the body consciousness, we are able to release the stories that have been held in our physical form and experience ourselves in a new light. This exploration allows us to go beyond the awareness of the form (eyes for seeing, ears for hearing) to realize the body's intelligence (consciousness produces thought, thought produces signals, signals catalyze reactions, reactions manifest form, form incarnates all). As our awareness expands, we are able to embody our truth, bringing the body into a state of aliveness and fullness that was previously unavailable.

Using the same steps outlined above, take a few slow, deep breaths, and enter the room of the body. When you are ready, ask, "What message does this room want to share with me right now?" When you are ready, record your experiences, again connecting with the message and the uniqueness of this room.

I feel. I am more than just my emotions.

The emotional body is the source of our experiential lives. Our emotions dictate how we choose to experience the moment. It is in the emotional body that we program our expectations of life. Our fears and hopes reside in this space. We may avoid what we fear at all costs, and seek what we hope without realizing this underlying relationship to our actions.

As we live in the moment, we may identify our feelings and associate them with what we are experiencing. I am feeling "good," therefore, this moment is appealing. I am feeling "bad," therefore, something about this moment is not positive. When our feelings are unconscious, we may not have the opportunity to see this relationship; however, the feelings are there underneath the surface. The emotional body says, "I feel, therefore, I am."

Using the same steps, connect to the doorway to the room of your emotions. Record your experience of this entryway, again identifying anything that was surprising or unexpected.

The emotional body, when aligned with our inner source—love—is capable of accompanying us through all events. The ups and downs of life are ever-present as flow, nothing more and nothing less. Through the feeling of empathy, we come to experience a fuller understanding of others, without taking on their feelings. We can hold the space for them, and for ourselves, so that we are all gently supported, no matter what. The feelings of good and bad dissolve into an acceptance of what is. As we deepen this awareness of the emotional body, we find that, simply, we are all love.

Through love for ourselves, and others, we can transform the world. A tremendous opportunity arises when we are living from our heart centers and when we are able to unconditionally love ourselves. We may find that acknowledging other feelings is necessary, as we are all capable of feeling hurt, joy, pain, and relief. When we come to love that part of ourselves that is hurting, joyous, in pain, or relieved, we find that we are finally able to release those transient feelings to experience love in its infinite expression.

Using the same steps as noted above, take a few slow, deep breaths, and enter the room of your emotions. When you are ready ask, what message does this room want to share with me right now? Without judgment, after you've experienced the full expression of the room, record your experience.

Spirit flows through me. I am more than just my spirit.

As incarnated souls, we have all taken this journey to the Earth-plane. We have come to find, share, and experience something that can only be experienced here. Our physical form, thoughts, and emotions are a great part of the experience we seek to gain knowledge of ourselves more deeply as spiritual beings.

What is our spirit? It is our essence beyond the Earth-plane — that aspect of each of us that is connected to (or a part of) the Source. Spirit is the non-tangible aspect of our experience that allows us to live fully and deeply on this plane while connecting ethereally to other planes. As Spirit flows through each one of us, it is the Source of our connectedness to all things, on this plane and beyond. The spiritual body says, "I am connected to source, therefore, I am."

Using the steps described above, connect to the doorway to the room of Spirit. Record your experience of this entryway, again identifying that which was surprising or unexpected.

Spirit is truth, as Source is truth. Spirit has no hidden agenda, judgment, or perception, because spirit is about the perfection of all. Each event, experience, and person has a spiritual consciousness, which includes an innate perfection. Spirit is our ally in understanding our truth, our reason for being, and our Source. It is through spirit consciousness that we are able to align our experiences on this plane with a higher level of knowing and understanding. Through the lens of spiritual awakening, we can begin to see more clearly and know more deeply that we are perfect.

Spirit is our connection to all things. Through our spiritual body we can feel at ONE with all. By knowing Spirit, we know we are not alone and we are not the chosen few, but we are the empowered many who have every right to experience life from a place of grace and centeredness.

Using the same steps, take a few slow deep breaths, and enter the room of Spirit. When you are ready, ask, what message does this room want to share with me right now? After experiencing all that the room has to offer, record your experience, again connecting with the message and the uniqueness of this room.

I live fully and effortlessly in my Core. I AM.

Now that we have spent time coming to know each room, we seek now to gain a deeper understanding of the container, the home. As we experience ourselves more fully, as an integrated consciousness, we are able to access any one part of ourselves at any time. We can call upon our inner ability to love when we are in the space of someone hurting, our innate knowingness when faced with a decision, our physical strength when working in the world, and our ability to co-create in alignment with source truth when we surrender to Spirit.

When was the last time that you felt truly integrated, when you felt as if your mind, body, emotions, and spirit were in balance? For some it may have been so long ago that there is no conscious memory, but just take a moment and really feel what it must have felt like to be integrated.

As you connect with this feeling of integration, allow your senses to blend into a knowingness of this present moment as perfection. This is what it is like to live in the Core. Whether you are able to live here every day, or just imagine what it feels like, you can use the analogy of the home to explore more deeply your Core.

Take a moment and allow your consciousness to rest upon the breath. As you breathe in, bring your awareness to your chest rising and falling with the inhale and exhale. Allow yourself to live in the breath for a moment. All there is right now is you and your breath. This breath nourishes you and allows you to take all your fears, anxieties, feelings, and understandings and put them aside for a moment to experience yourself as essence, just as you ARE.

As you breathe, close your eyes and begin to visualize all the doorways you experienced in the previous exercises — the doorways of the mental, physical, emotional, and spiritual bodies. Are you able to connect with all the doorways at once, or is only one present in this moment? If there is a doorway out of "view," is there a way to bring it into your awareness without losing the other doorways?

When you feel each doorway is present in your awareness, simultaneously open them all. Take a few moments to feel this opening. Can they all be opened at the same time? Explore with your senses this experience of having all rooms accessible to you, open to you. Is this effortless and comfortable, or is there resistance?

When you are ready, open your eyes and record your experience. Identify which doorways opened right away, which were exactly as you had previously experienced them, and which had changed. Allow yourself to connect to the experience without judgment. If one doorway was not ready to be opened, simply take note and do not become discouraged. Each step is an important one. As you access your own home, maybe for the first time, applaud yourself for taking on the challenge.

Our inner landscape may take on new forms as we find our way to the Core. Previously inaccessible or seemingly empty rooms may become available and filled. Rooms that were cluttered and disorganized may become manageable and open. We may even find that our rooms no longer exist. In their place is a single, integrated experience of life — our home has become a loft —open, expansive, and without boundaries.

When living in the Core, we can organize and reorganize ourselves and our inner landscape at will, creating the space for what we want to create in our lives, allowing our internal home to reflect our true values and knowingness. Effortlessly, we release what no longer serves us. We transform the baggage in the closet from an old wound into a trophy. We take out the libraries and compendiums of beliefs that are stored on bookshelves, annotated on photographs, and written in graffiti on the walls, and replace them with the messages of our truth, allowing perception and illusions to fade away so that we can see more clearly. With each shift we are deepening our connection to our Core, our inner landscape is clearing, and we are left only with what *is*. We release judgment and allow ourselves to be free, realizing that I AM is all there is.

Again taking a few deep, slow breaths, close your eyes and bring yourself into the space of your home. As you connect with this space, allow the doorways to remain in whatever state is comfortable. If they are opened or closed, it does not matter for the moment. Allow yourself to feel that you are home. With each inhale, repeat to yourself, "I am home, and with each exhale say, I have arrived. I am home, I have arrived. This is my home, I have arrived. This is perfection, I have arrived."

Now, slowly allow your awareness to open and bring the walls of each room "down." Allow the walls to dissolve, creating a single open space within your home. Know that you are safe in this space, that everything that you love is here, and anything that you fear can be transmuted. You are present and aware in this space. This space has its own intelligence, so if there is a question you need to ask, here is where you can find the answers. This is your Core.

When you are ready, open your eyes and record your experience. Was this Core what you expected? Was it challenging to dissolve the walls? Were the doors still present without the walls? Was it easy to stand in this space and see what was around you? Was there anyone else in the space with you? Did you ask a question and receive an answer?

Coming to know your Core is the first step to living there. Now that you have experienced your Core, what's next? Create a weekly or daily ritual of visiting your Core and observing where you are in your home, where things are shifting and realigning, and where change is not observable. Become curious about this space, identifying its objects, metaphors, and intelligence. If you don't know where to begin, you can ask, "What should I experience right now that is for my highest good?" and allow whatever is there to present itself to you. You may find that one day you are shown an aspect of yourself that is strong, supportive, and loving, and the next day it may be the opposite. Embrace and nourish each of these, as they are each aspects of you. In deepening this understanding, you are able to integrate it more gently.

If working with the Core is challenging, create a practice of working within each room. If you don't know where to begin, intuitively select a room and ask for guidance. As your awareness of each room increases, try to incorporate that room into your Core space.

Living fully and deeply in your truth through integrating the mental, emotional, physical, and spiritual bodies is living in the Core. The Core is the space in which these bodies are no longer separated. In the Core, each is present, accessible, and balanced within you. Your Core is wise, loving, and nonjudgmental. As you journey along your path to ascension, it is through living in *your* Core that a deepening connection with highest consciousness is available to *you*. Enjoy the opportunity to come to know yourself and your truth more deeply, and allow the experience to be gentle.

About Kimberly James

Kimberly James is a Certified Empowerment Coach, Energy Worker, and Holistic Educator. Kimberly specializes in allowing her clients to connect with their inner ability to create the reality that they deserve effortlessly. Kimberly integrates a variety of modalities, including Reiki, Shamanism, Crystal Healing, Coaching, Meditation, Mindfulness, and Intuition, to provide clients and students with the tools necessary to know creation as a way of being. For more information on Kimberly's practice and to find out how to work more deeply with your Core visit http://www.e2creation.com

CHAPTER 4

Preparing the Body to Receive and Maintain Ascension Energy

Belinda Kelly

The human body is more than just a compilation of water and minerals. Our bodies are governed by electrical, chemical, magnetic, and vibrational forces both within and outside of the physical form. Like everything in the universe, every organ and tissue in your body has its own unique vibrational frequency or tone. Combined with your denser physical frequencies are the frequencies of your subtle energy field or etheric body. Together, the physical and etheric bodies create a unique vibrational field or symphony that is *you*.

Just as no two snowflakes are the same, no two people will have the exact same vibrational symphony. This symphony is the energy marker of your soul; *it is your soul name*. When we are in optimal health, the symphony is vibrating at an optimal level and we are able to receive higher frequencies from our etheric body and incorporate them into our being. These higher frequencies then can resonate and harmonize with our symphony, bringing us into not only greater health but also into higher states of consciousness to support our ascension journey.

The subtle energy field supplies the life force to all living things. This phenomenon was first observed in the 1940s, when a German scientist found a way to photograph the electrical field around living plants, using Kirlian photography, or electrophotography. He photographed a leaf and was able to capture the discharge pattern. It was an exact image of the leaf. He then cut the leaf in half and destroyed the top half. The resulting photo still showed the same complete leaf. This field is the template for the leaf, just as our etheric body is the template for our bodies. Science has yet to explain how embryonic cells migrate spatially as the fetus is forming. How does a toenail cell know where to go? It is the etheric body that has the blueprint. Deepak Chopra, M.D. refers to this as the "quantum mechanical human body." He writes:

"Physics informs us that the basic fabric of nature lies at the quantum level, far beyond atoms and molecules. A quantum, defined as the basic unit of matter or energy, is from 10,000,000 to 100,000,000 times smaller than the smallest atom. At this level, matter and energy become interchangeable. All quanta are made of invisible vibrations—ghosts of energy—waiting to take physical form. Ayurveda says that the same is true of the human body—it first takes form as intense but invisible vibrations called quantum fluctuations, before it proceeds to coalesce into impulses of energy and particles of matter."[1]

This life force is what acupuncture is based on. Practitioners believe the life force, or qi, is carried through the body by specific channels and can be accessed through the meridian system. There are 12 major meridians which are named by the major organ they pass through. The goal of acupuncture is to clear blockages in the energy flow, thus allowing healing.

To further understand the connection between energy and our body's health, let us look at the body's composition. Water is the main element of our body. The spaces between the cells are composed of water and minerals, specifically silica. Water + Silica = Crystal. Crystals are used to transmit radio waves and they hold certain frequencies. Our body is a living, pulsating, liquid crystal that is able to emit energy waves and receive energy information. But like any radio, we have to have an energy source and be tuned to the right station. If we become dehydrated, we cannot carry the electrical pulses through our bodies. Water is a conductor of electricity and so are minerals. Minerals are more important than vitamins since every vitamin has a mineral that carries it through the body. Mineral deficiency is rampant in our society because our soils have been over-planted and our plants contain less of the minerals than they did even 30 years ago.

The energy which comes from food is as important as the nutrients it contains. In order to keep our body's frequencies at the optimal level we must eat the foods with the highest vibrational frequencies. These are fruits and vegetables. Sprouts of all types are also excellent choices because they contain the potential energy of the whole plant. Animal proteins have the lowest frequencies while sugar, artificial ingredients and pharmaceuticals actually alter our frequencies. Cooking not only lowers the vitamin and enzyme content of foods but also lowers the food's vibrational frequencies. This is why raw fruits and vegetables have the highest energy levels. A diet of raw fruits and vegetables is a wonderful way to cleanse the body, but for long-term health there should also be balance.

We must maintain our connection with the earth's frequency. A diet of just fruits and vegetables can raise our frequencies to the point where we lose that connection, and we are no longer grounded. The opposite is true of a diet that contains too many animal proteins. These foods lower our frequencies to the point where we cannot "hear" the higher frequencies. They bind us to the earth and keep us bound in the root chakra. Constipation will also do this. It is important to have at least two or more bowel movements a day so that energy of our waste does not "drag us down."

Food that is microwaved has energy that is totally altered as can be seen by Kirlian photography. Not only does microwaving create distorted energy fields, it also creates altered proteins that have never been seen in nature. There was an experiment done by a sixth-grade girl. She had two identical plants with two identical soils but one plant was fed with boiled water and the other was fed with microwaved water. The plant fed with microwaved water died in 10 days while the other plant thrived.

Many of our foods are being irradiated before they even reach the store. Genetically modified foods also have altered genes; some manufacturers are even combining plant and animal genes. What kind of energy fields will these "Frankenstein" foods have? Organically grown foods have the natural energy patterns the food was meant to have as well as all the micronutrients we need for optimal health.

It is not just the vitamins and minerals in our food that supply us with energy. Studies have shown that if you measured and weighed all the food given to a baby and then weighed and measured the sweat, urine and feces of that child you would come up with the same amount. Yet that child will gain weight and inches and develop mentally and emotionally. Similarly, if you take a corn seed and plant it in a pot with 10 pounds of soil and over time you add 5 pounds of water, you will get a plant that weighs 15 pounds and produces 5 pounds of corn with no soil loss. How is this possible? It is because, in both cases, the energy from the sun and earth is used as well as the energy and nutrients from food.

The energy that we receive from the etheric body follows a natural progression through the seven energy centers in our body known as chakras. These centers are often compared to transformers that receive the higher frequencies from the etheric body and step them down to be distributed throughout the body. The lower energies are at the base of the spine while the highest energies are at the crown of our heads. Each chakra's importance and functions are equal. We need both the lower and higher frequencies flowing through our body for health and well-being and to support our spiritual journey.

The chakras are each associated with a color that shows the progression of this energy. The root chakra is associated with the color red, the lowest frequency of light that we see. The color frequencies then move up to orange, the navel chakra; yellow, the solar plexus chakra; green, the heart chakra; blue, the throat chakra; indigo, the third eye chakra; and violet—the highest frequency we see, the crown chakra.

Each of these energy centers is also associated with an endocrine gland. Endocrine glands are ductless glands that secrete hormones. These hormones travel throughout the body and carry instructions for the organs. The endocrine glands work in harmony with each other; therefore, if any single gland is not functioning properly it can affect one or more of the other glands. The energy we receive flows through the chakra system, then through the endocrine glands, and then through the entire body.

The root chakra is located at the base of the spine and is linked to the adrenal glands. Your adrenal glands are your stress glands or your survival glands. They are responsible for our "fight or flight" response. We have all heard the stories of the mother who lifted a car off of her baby, or the man who scaled a tree when attacked by a bear. This is the adrenals responding to a major stressor. When we are faced with stress on a daily basis, from whatever source, we fatigue our adrenals. Just as each of our chakras can prevent the flow of energy to the others, the adrenals can affect other endocrine glands. A sudden emotional trauma can also cause the adrenals to shut down the thyroid gland. The adrenals can become so fatigued that the "fight or flight" response is triggered needlessly. This is what causes anxiety and even panic attacks.

We need to reduce the stressors in our life, especially the pressures we put on ourselves. To heal the adrenals we need eight hours of sleep at night, preferably between 10 pm and 6 am. Licorice root will feed the adrenals, but if you have a potassium imbalance it may raise the blood pressure. Rhodiola will feed the adrenals and reduce stress. Gotu kola, L-Theanine, 5-HTP, vitamin B5, passion flower and valerian root are some good choices for adrenal health.

The navel chakra is located just above the navel and is associated with the ovaries in women and the testes in men. The sex hormones are related to development and growth as well as fertility. An imbalance in this area can lead to abnormal development and infertility. During puberty the body produces hormones that signal the body to stop growth. This is why it is important to keep the hormones balanced even in young people. Red raspberry is wonderful for young women while saw palmetto works well for young men. Herbs for fertility in women include maca, red raspberry, dong quai and wild yam. Men can use saw palmetto, maca and the amino acid l-carnitine.

The solar plexus chakra is located just below the chest cavity and is also associated with the adrenal glands. The adrenal glands have two different functions and develop from two different tissues. The medulla produces adrenaline and other related hormones while the cortex produces corticosteroids. Thus the medulla is affected by the root chakra while the cortex is linked with the solar plexus chakra.

The adrenals are responsible for hormone production especially after menopause in women or andropause in men. Menopausal symptoms are not normal! Testosterone loss in men is not normal! During our fertile years the ovaries and testes are an extra source of hormones, so man can be fertile even under stress. After fertility the ovaries and testes do not need to produce extra hormones so we go directly to our adrenals for our hormones. If you are experiencing menopausal or andropause symptoms, you need to feed the adrenal glands.

The adrenals are also active in blood sugar regulation. A perfect example is the person who is given large amounts of steroid medication and suddenly his blood sugar goes sky high. He is now called a diabetic and put on more medication. Steroids shut down the adrenal cortex which is responsible for signaling the pancreas to produce insulin. Because of this relationship between the adrenals and blood sugar regulation some writings suggest the pancreas is the endocrine gland for the solar plexus.

All of the herbs mentioned for the root chakra are good for the adrenal cortex also. Glandulars work especially well for the cortex. A glandular formula uses small amounts of bovine or porcine gland to carry the DNA of that particular gland to the body. It also works on an energetic level to give the proper energy frequency of the gland. Hormone precursors also help the adrenals rest while bringing the hormone levels up. DHEA and pregnenolone can be used for men and women. Black cohosh can help with hot flashes, but if you stop taking it and the adrenals are still weak, they will come back.

The heart chakra is the first of the higher vibrational chakras. Each chakra above the solar plexus is associated with two adrenal glands. We can speculate that the frequencies at this level need two glands to transform the energy from the etheric body to the physical body. The heart chakra is located in the center of the chest and is associated with the heart and the thymus gland. Yes, the heart is an endocrine gland. It has only recently been discovered that the heart actually makes hormones but not much is known about how they work. Hormones have been found in tears and they are different when we are crying with laughter then when we are crying with sadness. Could these be the hormones of happiness and sadness?

The thymus gland is one of the major glands of the immune system. It has been well-documented that immune function is depressed during grief, thus the emotional connection with the thymus gland. In infancy this gland is responsible for developing the natural defense mechanisms we have to fight pathogens. Because most older people have atrophied thymus glands it was thought that this was only important in young children. We now know that keeping the thymus healthy keeps the immune system operating at optimal levels. Immune function can be enhanced with cat's claw, astragalus, medicinal mushrooms and vitamin C.

We have been seeing an increasing number of people with heart disease in the last few decades. Energies that are blocked at the lower level can lead to blockages of the heart. Herbs for the heart include hawthorn berry, cayenne and ginko biloba. Vitamin E, CoQ10 and ribose are also good for heart function.

The throat chakra is located just above the Adams apple and is connected to the thyroid and parathyroid gland. The thyroid gland is responsible for regulation of our metabolism. A weak thyroid gland will produce weight gain, dry skin, loss of hair and depression. Low thyroid function can also affect hormone level because of the connection to the adrenal glands. Thyroid deficiency is very common today. Aspartame will suppress thyroid function as will systemic yeast infections. When yeast in our bodies goes systemic it has an affinity for the thyroid. A lack of good bacteria in the body is what allows yeast to leave the gut and go systemic. In the fifties and sixties mothers were told that nursing was not necessary because formulas were better than breast milk. Breast milk is the source of the good bacteria the infant needs to form the colony that is vital to the immune system. Without it there is no natural protection from the yeast that occurs in our colons. Add to that the overuse of antibiotics that kill our good bacteria as well as the bad and we have an epidemic of yeast-related illnesses.

The parathyroid is actually four small glands found in the thyroid. The parathyroid is responsible for maintaining the proper calcium levels in the blood. Over-activity of the parathyroid, one of the most under diagnosed disorders, will result in osteoporosis. Any remedy that helps the thyroid also will help the parathyroid.

The major herb for the thyroid is kelp. It is a natural source of iodine which the thyroid needs to function. If there is a blockage in the chakra above or below the heart chakra, this can create a spillage of energy which then causes an overactive condition. An overactive thyroid, or a thyroid that is working at a higher vibrational frequency, needs bugleweed. Unlike popular belief, kelp is also needed to feed an overactive thyroid since the natural source of vitamins and minerals cannot over stimulate a gland. The body will not absorb what it does not need.

The third eye chakra is located in the middle of the forehead and is associated with the pituitary gland and the hypothalamus. Like the adrenal glands, the pituitary is another gland that forms from two different types of tissue and is under two different control systems. The anterior portion of the pituitary is the gland of the third eye and the posterior portion is involved with the crown chakra. The third eye chakra is the center of our intuition or inner vision. The pituitary is known as a master gland because it produces hormones to regulate all the glands in the body. Small growths on it can affect other glands. Also, a lack of amino acids can slow the pituitary's function. Sanicle is the herb to clear the pituitary gland.

Just above the anterior pituitary is the hypothalamus gland. This gland is the regulator of all the glands as well as the autonomic nervous system. The hypothalamus receives information from all the senses and the nervous system, and then coordinates the data to regulate responses in the body. It is also responsible for our mood and behavior, hunger, thirst, body temperature, water balance, metabolism, blood pressure and more—it is the brain's brain. Dysfunction of the hypothalamus can lead to psychotic disorders as well as suppressed function of all the endocrine system. Alfalfa is the herb for the hypothalamus. Stroke or tumors can also affect this gland. Cayenne pepper or capsicum given every 15 minutes at the first sign of a stroke will minimize the damage to the brain. Growths or tumors respond well to greasewood, whole apricot, paw paw and essiac tea.

The crown chakra is at the top of the head and is associated with the pineal gland and the posterior pituitary. This is the highest frequency in the body and is our connection to the higher energies. The pineal gland also produces a high degree of calcium crystals often referred to as "brain sand." These crystals are what promote the reception of the higher energies. We have a receiver in our brains! These energies enter the crown chakra as white light which contains all the frequencies and colors of the spectrum. This is then filtered through the individual chakras and distributed through the body.

One of the most toxic chemicals to the pineal gland is fluoride. Because of the calcium content of the pineal gland it will accumulate fluoride. It has been found to have more toxic fluoride than bones or teeth.[2] The naturally occurring fluoride is calcium fluoride but the fluoride used in our water and toothpaste is sodium fluoride, a toxic synthetic chemical.

As the pineal is another master gland, it can disrupt hormone function in other glands. Sunlight is essential for the pineal, and must enter our eyes to stimulate this gland. Melatonin, our sleep hormone, is the major hormone of this gland. Waking at night or having trouble falling asleep is a symptom of pineal dysfunction. Working at night and sleeping during the day will disrupt the natural rhythms of our body and effect the pineal. Melatonin can be taken to help regulate the pineal. When melatonin is used, it often makes meditations, especially the next morning, more enlightening.

The crown and the third eye chakra are interrelated through the connection with the anterior pituitary. When the crown and the third eye chakra are open they create a polarity that allows the third eye to open to higher vibrations. This is the center of our spirituality and our connection to the Creator. The pituitary provides the balanced integration of logic with the spiritual vision of the pineal.

Each chakra is also associated with certain traits and emotions. The root chakra is our link to the earth's energy. It is associated with survival and creativity; anger and hatred are the negative emotions.

The navel chakra is responsible for our emotional development. When this chakra is in balance it is associated with joy and pleasure while feelings of abandonment and rejection are the unhealthy emotions associated with it.

The solar plexus chakra is the seat of our will or personal power; the opposite traits are guilt, low self-esteem and powerlessness.

When we move to the higher colors we move into higher emotions and frequencies that can connect us to the Creator or the Ascension Energy. The heart chakra is our center of love and compassion. An imbalance in this area often shows as fear of rejection or ridicule. This energy center is where the energy of the soul is anchored and is the bridge between the upper and lower frequencies.

The throat chakra is our center for truth and communication. Denial is the negative emotion associated with it.

The third eye chakra is our center for intuition, while confusion and depression can indicate an imbalance in this area.

The crown chakra is our spiritual connection. Any imbalance in the other chakras can affect the crown chakra, and thus our mind and soul connection to the spiritual body. This is why negative emotions and thoughts affect our health by changing our vibrational energies. Maintaining the emotions of compassion and love and gratitude in our thoughts as well as our words will raise our vibrational frequencies.

In addition to good nutrition, proper rest, stress elimination, and supplementation with herbs and vitamins, there are other things we can do to achieve balance in our bodies and to prepare us to receive higher energies.

Flower remedies are excellent for emotional healing. They are homeopathic remedies created from flowers which work on the physical as well as the etheric body.

Traditional homeopathic remedies are also invaluable because they too work at the etheric level. Most dis-ease starts in the etheric body by a change in the vibrational frequency that then moves down into the physical body. By healing at the etheric level we often get profound results. Herbal remedies and vitamin therapy work at the physical level, and if combined with homeopathic or flower remedies, we often get a balance between the physical and etheric bodies more quickly.

Electromagnetic fields disrupt our subtle energy fields. These disrupters include high tension power lines, televisions, computers, electric blankets, cell phones and satellite transmissions. These fields shift the polarity and the rotation of the energy of our bodies and can lead to ill health. We cannot eliminate this electromagnetic chaos completely, but we can reverse our polarity simply by rubbing the abdomen in a clockwise motion with the right hand for a few minutes. You are literally pulling the body's field back into a clockwise motion.

Meditation is a way to help open the third eye and crown chakra and release stressors that are locked in the body. When we meditate or quiet our mind, we create a communication between our physical body and our spiritual self. Over time we become more aware of the emotion behind the blockages. Through frequent meditation we can release the blockages in our chakra system that hamper the flow of energy to the crown chakra.

All consciousness is connected through the etheric energy field, thus as we achieve balance in our own bodies we help all of humanity on its path of ascension. Man's evolution is a progression through the chakra system. Early man lived in the root chakra where survival was the main concern. When agriculture was established we began to form communities and relationships. This was a move up into the navel chakra as our frequencies increased. As communities developed into cities and nations, we had leaders and even nations striving for power and position. This brought us to the solar plexus chakra. As consciousness developed and we began to have compassion for others, respect for the earth and ourselves, our vibrational frequencies increased to move us up through the higher frequencies of our energy centers. This shows the interconnection between all beings.

Humanity is now moving into the energy of the heart chakra, the bridge between the physical and spiritual centers. By letting go of old fears and maintaining the energy of love, compassion and gratitude, we make the transition from purely physical beings to spiritual beings living a physical life. Every individual that can access and maintain the higher frequencies assists in raising the consciousness of the planet as a whole.

About Belinda Kelly

Belinda Kelly, N.D.,C.N.C. is a Board Certified Medical Naturopath, Certified Nutritional Consultant, Master Iridologist and Certified Natural Health Professional. She is a member of the American Association of Medical Naturopaths, The International Association of Holistic Iridology and The American Association of Nutritional Consultants. She has been working with herbs and natural therapies for over twenty years. Belinda is currently the owner of Kelly's Herb House, a natural health store featuring Iris Analysis,

Muscle Response Testing, Yoga, Pilates, Reiki, Massage, Ionic Foot Baths and Middle Eastern Dance.

The web address is www.kellysherb.com. Or you may contact the store directly at:

>Kelly's Herb House
>401 Headquarters Dr.
>Suite 102
>Millersville, MD 21108
>410-729-4321

Every Step is Holy

The journey from known
to unknown, from the
unreal to the real, is rarely
revealed in advance.
The potholes, detours,
false starts, and quick
retreats are each honorable,
and even needed in the bigger
scheme, in the forest that can't
be seen between the trees.

It took years for me to realize
that the very twists and turns
and shadows I labeled "problems"
were really sacred ground,
grace disguised as obstacles,
the whole path a pilgrimage,
mysteries baring themselves
before me all along the way.

Danna Faulds, *From Root to Bloom*

CHAPTER 5

Answering the Call

Toni Neal

For as long as I can remember, I have had a deep curiosity about the meaning, the purpose of life; a desire to know not only why we are here, but what awaits us beyond death. I wasn't raised with a strong dedication to any particular religion, for which I am now grateful, so it was easy for me to delve into "the mysteries" of ancient wisdom teachings and mysticism. The teachings of Hinduism, Buddhism, and the Tao Te Ching – they all resonated with me and I have always felt a strong connection with Jesus. My search for "the Truth" intensified and waned at times; the one thing it never did was to go away. This intense longing, yearning, I now recognize as "the call to awaken"; another way to describe it may be the "call to Ascension."

One of my earliest memories is from when I was a young child of probably no more than ten. We lived in a rather isolated area with few playmates; again, one of those things that I now see as a blessing in disguise. I was introspective by nature, and one day I thought, "What would it be like if there was no creation?" I might not have used that exact word, but to my child's mind, this meant everything in the world of form. So, I began to mentally subtract everything I could see or think of - people, trees, plants, animals, finally the sun, moon and stars. What was left? Nothing – what I sensed as blackness, emptiness. I think I got part of it right, anyway – the "nothingness." But it so terrified me that I vowed to never indulge in that kind of thinking again!

That was perhaps the closest I ever got, before an experience in the '90s, to glimpsing the truth. I was probably too young to understand that what I perceived as "nothing" was the very essence of all that is. And yet, it made such an impact on me, obviously, that I never forgot it.

In the Bible in Ephesians 5:14 St. Paul says, "…Awake thou, that sleepest, arise from the dead, and Christ will give thee light." Most of us, until we have felt that initial stirring from within, are like sleepwalkers, or to be truthful, more like zombies. We go through life on automatic pilot, taking on the beliefs and attitudes of our families, society, culture, never questioning but content to live out our little life here the best we can. That usually means whatever is acceptable in the eyes of others. We strive for success in the world; we are happy for a while if we "make it," and feel unworthy if we don't. Any happiness that we do achieve is usually short-lived or comes with so many problems attached that we wonder if we weren't better off before!

My own life followed this pattern. I reached a certain level in my career after 19 years, and one day I stopped and thought, "Is this all there is? I work to make more money, to buy more things, bigger things, better things – where does it stop? And more importantly, where is the joy?" I felt that life was passing me by. That isn't to say that I hated my job; in fact, it was very interesting work, but deep down I felt that I just didn't fit there anymore. I experienced a feeling of isolation, a deep, spiritual discontent.

Some people are able to follow this inner wisdom and make an abrupt shift in their life situation. Others, like me, need a little extra coaching; mine came in the form of illness. Having a very supportive husband allowed me to finally come to terms with all of this, and I left my career to work at home.

This marked a turning point in my life. Within a year I had a whole new life, new interests, and yes, I even found a non-denominational church filled with people with similar beliefs. My health issues had led me to alternative medicine, energy and spiritual healing, and a new network of friends. As I look back now I can see how each step led to something else, and how important each one was to the whole.

One thing that has become clear is that nothing, regardless of how wonderful and fulfilling it may be, lasts in this realm. Impermanence is the very nature of things, and that includes all of the forms my path has taken. However, in the mid -'90s I had a spiritual experience in which I got a glimpse, however small, of something greater; of that which never changes and yet is here with us even now in this world of form. The details of my experience aren't important. What is important is the undeniable peace and feeling of "rightness" with everything just the way it is, that came with it. It was as if I had awakened from a deep sleep, and I felt what can be best described as a loving Presence that is ever with me. The most significant thing that I realized was that this Presence had *always* been with me and with everyone, even though we knew it not. Yes, the experience faded, but I've never forgotten that sense of peace and the Presence which I now understand to be the tangible form of that which had been calling me all along – my own Higher Self.

All of us will eventually respond to that inner calling. Like the prodigal son, we will come to our senses and begin the journey home. Our journey's focus shifts from outward, in the world, to an inward or upward journey. This doesn't mean everything will suddenly be easy and swift from then on. On the contrary, this is when things really get interesting! The last thing our ego - our sense of a separate self or identity - wants is for us to make this choice. And so the fun and games begin! This is when we really see what St. Paul meant by "dying daily." Our ego does not go away gently into the night. As we begin our steps on the road to self-realization, all that is holding us back will be brought to our awareness. Feelings of unworthiness, inferiority, guilt, and judgments - all rear their ugly heads and we may shrink back, hoping they will go away. We may delay the process, but once begun, there is no turning back.

At some point, whether in this or another lifetime, we make a pivotal decision, I believe, to really get serious about getting serious. We may have dabbled with spirituality, read all the "right" books, attended all the latest self-help workshops, and learned how to meditate. But our good intentions are not enough. To really go further, a lot more is asked of us and we really have to decide if awakening is what our heart wants *above all else.*

I can remember two specific instances when I made that decision, although I didn't really understand the full significance at the time. The first was made as a result of chronic health issues that plagued me, and I decided to find the *answer to health*, not having a clue where that decision would ultimately lead. The second decision came after years of striving for happiness only to find dissatisfaction once again. This time I decided that *peace of mind* was what I wanted above all else. I think my spiritual guides and angels must have leaped for joy when they heard that! "Finally, she's beginning to understand!" As a result of these decisions, I was led to teachings by an American mystic and spiritual healer who lived in the 20th century – Joel Goldsmith, and ultimately to *A Course In Miracles*, a modern-day channeled teaching of Jesus. I found so many similarities in their messages and felt that certain "yes" when you realize you are reading Truth; I knew I had found my path.

After having been on this new journey for some years, we may look back at our former life and not even recognize the person that we were before. Certainly, our life circumstances may have changed as our priorities shifted. But each person's path is uniquely suited to them, and we can save ourselves a lot of wasted time and unnecessary suffering that comes from comparing our path to someone else's, feeling not quite as "spiritual."

How I longed to have visions when I meditated! Or to hear a voice, telling me what I should do. This is not the way I receive guidance. I had a three-year period when it was as if I had my very own muse whispering beautiful music and Truth-filled passages in my ear, which I struggled to write down – and realized that must have been the reason I learned to play the piano – just to be able to write the music! But it takes years to develop trust that we are being guided by a Higher Power; that we have spiritual guides and helpers who do know exactly what is right for us, what we can accept and the way we can accept it.

We may finally accept the uniqueness of our own path, but it may take a long time before we realize that this means we have to give up judging everyone else's path as well! How can we possibly know what is right for someone else – what their soul needs for growth? This is particularly difficult when you have children or loved ones that are suffering in some way. We want to keep them from experiencing pain, and yet hasn't it been our own pain that has brought some of the greatest lessons? Recognizing that only Spirit knows what is best and acknowledging that that same Spirit is guiding us all, will not only help to reestablish peace within yourself, but is also one of the greatest gifts you can offer anyone.

Sometimes we are led in a certain direction only for a short while – perhaps there are people there we need to meet - and then we move on. This applies not just to what we may think of as our spiritual path, but to everyday life situations. We begin to realize that we can't compartmentalize what is spiritual and what isn't; our whole life becomes dedicated to this Higher calling, and everything is part of it.

Yes, trust is essential on this journey. And yet even the mystics experienced the dark night of the soul, those times when we feel cut off from our Source, from our guidance. This can be a very bleak time unless we understand that it, too, serves a purpose. This may be a time for us to assimilate and put into practice all that we have learned. Sometimes we feel like we are in a holding pattern, waiting, waiting, for we don't know what. When we recognize these times, it can help if we surrender with "may this serve a higher purpose," or, "this, too, shall pass." Nonresistance is another key that helps immeasurably when we remember to use it.

Some, but not necessarily all who dedicate their life to this purpose may experience tremendous upheavals in their life. This can at times be very painful as everything we value and believe is called into question. We may feel that we are being called upon to make great sacrifices by choosing this path and wonder if it is worth it. Or we may feel guilty that we have created disharmony when our goal is peace. We may even feel we are being punished.

It is helpful at such times to realize that what is occurring is part of a larger picture. As changes take place in our consciousness, it is only natural that this will be reflected in our life. As time passes we can look back and see that these difficult times were necessary for our growth, and our faith in the process deepens. They may have been necessary for sorting out what was truly important and what wasn't. As we let go of our attachments and old beliefs a great burden is lifted from us; we feel lighter and freer.

Taking responsibility for our life and holding ourselves accountable are essential on this path. This means giving up the role of victim and acknowledging the part that we have played in whatever appears to be taking away our peace. When we begin to see the part that we have played in creating some drama, and we can be *very* creative, there may be a tendency to feel guilty. "I should have known better! Haven't I been studying this for so long?" etc. But that is just another ego ploy to keep us stuck. Forgiveness, a crucial factor on this journey, must include forgiveness of ourselves.

How freeing it is when we recognize that we are the cause of our own pain! Now I don't mean, obviously, that people can't harm us physically or take advantage of us, or insult us. But only we can decide how to respond both outwardly and internally. When we recognize that only *we* determine how we feel, that the pain has nothing to do with the other person or situation, then we know only *we* can effect a change.

For years I had boundary issues with certain people in my life. I felt controlled, manipulated and I was very angry, although I buried this anger deep inside. But life always gives you what you need to grow. And usually in a more intense way until you finally learn the lesson. So years later another person enters my life, a person who obviously had boundary issues by anyone's standards! Things reached a climax and suddenly I recognized something familiar about this situation. I was extremely uncomfortable, but underneath was a lot of anger and I thought, "When have I felt this way before?" Immediately the other individuals from my past who had evoked similar feelings came to mind.

But now I was coming from a different place. I realized the anger that I had was really not toward the other person at all, but toward myself! I was angry that *I* had not been able to establish healthy boundaries in this relationship, to have enough self-respect to say "no." I realized what a gift this person had given me – reflecting my own issues that I needed to come to terms with. The outcome was that I was finally able to end the relationship in the most loving way I could for all parties concerned. I recognized a great healing had taken place as I was able to extend this same understanding to the other people from my past, releasing them and forgiving them and myself.

Paying attention to our thoughts, our feelings and our need to react are crucial on this journey. A reaction that is out of proportion to the situation is a red flag that a button has been pushed, meaning, something we need to look at in ourselves. I like to imagine a little doll with a lot of buttons representing different emotions such as anger, resentment, joy, fear, happiness. When someone pushes one of our buttons, it is easy to put the blame on them. But if we hadn't *had* the button, it couldn't have *been* pushed, could it? Wouldn't it be nice instead to imagine pushing another button, a default button: restore to the original manufacturer's settings -PEACE!

As I mentioned above, when I recognize a familiarity about an uncomfortable feeling or emotion, this is a clue for me that it is not the present situation or person that is the cause. When I can get in touch with the feeling, I am usually able to remember other situations where I felt the same way. This helps me to see the underlying issue, or content which is the same in all of the cases, just in a different form. It is there to show me some underlying belief I am holding that needs to be reevaluated. It is also helpful to realize that when things resurface, it is because we are now at a point to heal at a higher level. So we become the witness, the observer of our thoughts and our feelings, using the wisdom that we have gained to discern what no longer serves us, and release it. But being a witness is not the same as being a judge. We must always be gentle and loving with ourselves.

There are so many paradoxes on the spiritual path. We are going forward and yet we are going back to Source. We are growing into the Self that we always were. We can only walk our own path, and each must make his own way and yet we have all of the help in the Universe available to us. And each part contributes to the whole. Obstacles turn into doorways to deeper truths. And finally, one of the greatest paradoxes is the belief that *we* must *do* something for enlightenment, awakening to occur. All of our doing, all of our thinking can only take us so far. It is our willingness to let go of all our beliefs, and the understanding that we cannot do anything of ourselves, that will free us. To awaken to our true nature, to discover the "nothingness," the true essence of all that Is – this is our destiny. Are we ready to answer the call?

About Toni Neal

Toni Neal lives in Pasadena, Maryland, with Larry, her husband of 21 years. After working for the federal government for 19 years, she left and embarked on a new path which led to her becoming an ordained minister and a student/teacher of *A Course in Miracles*, and an herbalist. Toni works from her home as an editor and distributor and assists her husband in the production of his music. Her other interests include writing, composing music, playing folk harp, gardening and spending time with her grandchildren. She can be contacted at tonilneal@comcast.net.

CHAPTER 6

Living Space to Sacred Space
Creating Transcendent Environments

Peter Jackson

"We shall not cease from exploration, and at the end of our exploring will be to arrive where we started and know the place for the first time." T.S. Elliot

"There is nothing in nature that does not symbolize something in the world of spirit." Swedenborg

Have you ever been in a building that felt cool and clammy and you couldn't wait to get out of there? How about a building or place outside that felt soothing and warm, and you didn't want to leave? Or homes where individuals experience chronic illnesses and you felt exhausted just being there? Why do houses occupied by a succession of different families over many years contract the same disease, yet there is no genetic association between families? Why do animals graze and rest in certain areas of a field but not in other areas that appear completely identical? Why do you feel weak, low in energy, or depressed in one place, but energized and happy in another? The Earth we live on is not the same from one location to another.

Our living and working locations are as diverse as the many people on this planet. Physical locations can promote health or illness. The space you occupy can influence your physical, emotional, mental, and spiritual well-being. This is the result of geophysical or gravitational forces and electrical or magnetic forces interacting with you, and the construction geometries of your living spaces. Our living locations are not the same from one location to another, even though they seem to be to the naked eye. In some locations, just a few yards in distance make a significant difference. There are tools you can use to alter the interactions of energetic forces to make your living space into a "conditioned" or sacred space that supports your journey to well-being and transcendence! We can change our living environments but a little background is important first.

Geopathic stress, from *Geo* meaning Earth, and *pathos*, a malady or pathology, as in *dis-ease*. Specific locations on the Earth and its natural and/or man-made structures in living and working environments induce stress in the physical body's biological processes, such as the immune system. You are a living system of energies that are not separate from the Earth and its energetic properties, be they harmonious or discordant to biological well-being.

To understand geopathic stress, consider this analogy. Rock boulders of different weight and size produce different speeds and heights of water waves when dropped into a lake. The speed and height of the wave indicates the amount of energy within the wave. Water waves radiate in all directions from the point of the boulder's impact on the water. When different waves intersect, they can combine to create larger, stronger waves. They either create harmonious and gentle interactions, or discordant and jolting interactions based on the geometry of their intersection. If you are on this lake, you are subject to harmonious or discordant wave affects. You may feel good in some wave intersections but ill or out of balance in other wave intersections.

Our Earth is threaded with "energy lines" and zones of energy similar to the human nerve complexes and acupuncture meridian system in which chi flows in the human body. These Earth zones and lines of force include static electrical forces, magnetic fields, and significant gravitational forces, which have a powerful influence on living beings. These inter-related energy fields are in dynamic motion above, on, and beneath the Earth. They move and propagate in vertical and/or horizontal directions. They follow laws of symmetry and direction in relation to the Earth's spherical geometry and geomagnetic field. From one location to another, the earth's magnetic field strength (measured in thousandths of a gauss or milligauss), ground water electrical conductivity, and emission of ionizing radiation such as radon gas will vary. Dr. Ernst Hartmann and Dr. Curry of the Bioclimatic Institute of Germany studied these energetic systems in the 20th century. These scientists found that energetic fields flow in and across the Earth in geometric grids. They also vary based on season, global location, planetary movements, and sun spot activity.

Data from researchers around the world reveals the causes of geopathic stress are natural and man-made. Yet we are just beginning to understand the implications of how geopathic stress influences our health and well-being. Geological fault lines, water courses, volcanic structures, gas lines, electrical/ power lines, and building geometries are contributory factors. These factors move in the Earth's gravitational field, which generates magnetic and electrical field affects. Near Croton, Connecticut is an Indian sacred site called the Cliff of Tears. Within a few yards on this site the geomagnetic field significantly varies from 330 milligauss at an 80 degree slope to 700 milligauss at a 59 degree slope. These are extremely high and unusual magnetic field changes. Typical readings of the earth's geomagnetic field at the earth's surface range from 0.3 to 2 milligauss. At the Cliff of Tears visitors frequently become depressed, their gums may bleed or nose bleeds occur for no obvious reason within short periods of time.

Dr. Ernst Hartmann is credited with the discovery of a global grid (now called the Hartmann Grid) associated with geopathic stress. He researched the effects of geopathic stress on humans for thirty years. His extensive report[1] documented that illnesses were influenced by geopathic stress at geographic locations. Prolonged and repetitive periods of living or working in geopathic stress zones stimulated predisposition to degenerative conditions. He documented a correlation between cancer and intersecting "Hartmann lines" where people slept or worked for long periods.

Constant slow movement of fault lines along earthquake zones contributes to geopathic stress. Discontinuities in geological structures such as thrusts, fractures and fissures in combination with subterranean water movement may result in geopathic stress zones at the surface. Geologic pressure within faults can affect the electrical field of mineral deposits. One example of this is piezoelectric quartz-bearing rock.

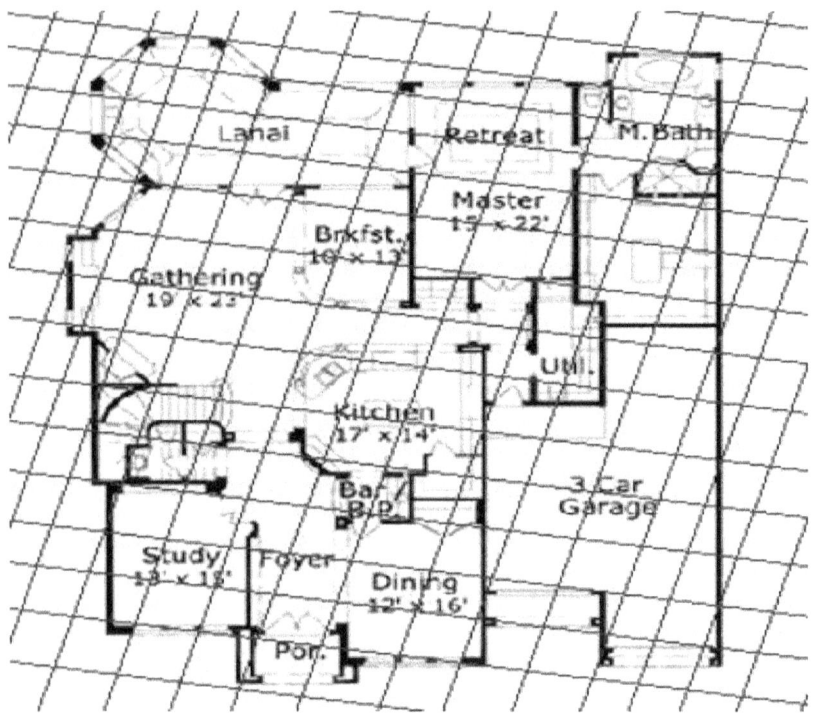

Example of geopathic lines (Hartman Grid) over a home floor plan. The intersections can be biologically destructive over the long term if individuals work or sleep over the intersections.

As water flows underground, it produces an electromagnetic field at microwave frequencies. This field fluctuates depending on mineral type and content. Dr. Hartmann and Dr. Dieter Ashcroft used a Genitron Felix-3 microwave frequency recorder to detect microwave frequencies of underground water movement.[2] European researchers have found that water flowing under a dwelling results in the residents feeling tired, prone to premature aging, and loss of vitality.

You can learn to eliminate the geopathic stress from living/working spaces or hire a "geobiologist." Geobiology is a European term for the art and science of using ancient as well as modern tools to locate and mitigate geopathic stress influences that cause biological disharmony to living organisms. The purpose is to create an environment that is conducive to healing, enhances creativity, and establishes a sacred space that supports you in achieving transcendent goals.

Until scientific detection systems are developed, dowsing is the primary tool for detecting geopathic stress. Every substance has a resonant energy signature, and each element a unique resonant signature which can be identified through spectrographic and magnetic resonance techniques. The physical body and its bioelectrical and electro-chemical processes are composed of these elements and their resonant energy signatures. You transmit and receive resonant energy patterns and information. Each of us can tune into resonant signatures in a manner similar to tuning a TV to our favorite channel. A dowser is naturally sensitive to nature's resonant energy signatures. Consciousness is the dowser's instrument for "tuning in" to the resonating signature of a substance. The dowser uses "L" rods or pendulums that are antennas for a subconscious response to the subtle resonant signatures of substances through neural-muscular reflex reaction. Dowsers have a long history in our culture.

Picture of L rods used in dowsing

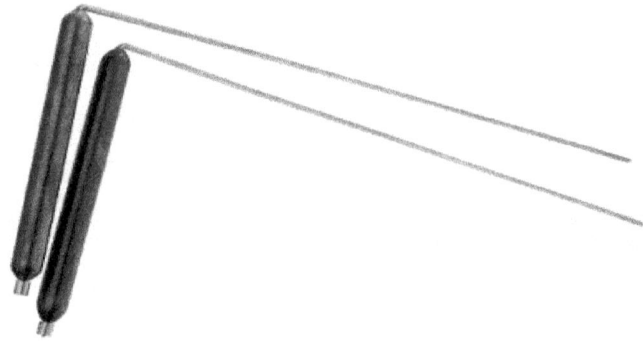

In 1910 dowsers discovered one of the greatest oilfields in California, Lakeview #1. This gusher shot oil 200 feet into the air and produced more than 100,000 barrels a day. The result was a collapse of oil prices by 65% for a short period of time.

Two German researchers, Winzer and Melzer, made a significant association of geological fault vein radiation to disease in the 1920s. They divided the German city of Stuttgart into districts of varying rates of cancer occurrence and attempted to correlate the disease to underground rock formations, but their attempt failed. However, when experienced dowsers advised them to investigate the five prominent geological fault lines that ran under the city, Winzer and Melzer found the faults ran directly beneath the districts with the highest rates of cancer mortality.[3] Decades later German and international researchers determined that many fault lines emanate forms of ionizing radiation that is hazardous to health. Today we call one form of that ionizing radiation radon gas.

In 1929, an expert German dowser named Baron Gustav Von Pohl claimed cancer was caused by "energy currents" located beneath sleeping locations.[4] The Mayor of the Vilsbiburg in Bavaria let him dowse houses in the town for energy currents. The energy line locations were compared with records of deceased cancer patients. The results showed a remarkable coincidence. Von Pohl later dowsed the City of Stetten for the same energy currents. Stetten's medical director stated that Von Pohl's earth currents ran beneath the beds of 5,348 people who died from cancer in the previous 21 years.

Geopathic stress is a serious health issue in Europe. Some medical specialists recommend that a geobiologist investigate the home before deciding on a course of therapy. Only a few examples are given herein due to space limitations; the reader is encouraged to do further research on this subject.[4]

The Vienna Report, Researching Biological Influences of Geopathic Stress (Consumer Research Institute, Product Marketing, Vienna, Austria, Sept. 1987 to Dec. 1988). The study's objective was to validate statistically if geopathic stress influences health. Geopathic stress locations were defined as: "Earth radiations evoked by a discontinuity of the normal physical parameters on the surface of the Earth," then shortened to "Disturbed Zones." The hypothesis was that geophysical characteristics of the Earth's surface are not uniform and location-dependent influences have detrimental effects on human biochemical systems.

Three expert dowsers located geopathic disturbed zones. Each dowser studied eight different locations and provided maps depicting disturbed zones and neutral zones with no geopathic stress. The neutral zones were used for double blind testing with study participants. Disturbed zones were related to underground streams, Hartmann grids, and geological faults. An independent electrical engineer surveyed each zone to rule out radio frequency broadcast influences. Healthy volunteer subjects, 20-35 years in age were screened. No volunteers were given information about the Disturbed and Neutral Zones. Biochemical investigations at the Disturbed and Neutral Zones were standardized to:

- Investigations after 15 minutes on Neutral Zone.

- Investigations after 15 minutes on the Disturbed Zone.

- Investigations again after another 15 minutes on the Neutral Zone.

Twenty-four biological parameters involving 985 volunteers provided 70,920 individual observed measurements. For all 24 parameters, 12 were significant to highly significant, 5 exhibited tendencies to significance, and 7 parameters proved negative. Of the 24 parameters 17 proved positive. A small sampling of significant parameters includes:

Heart Frequency Reaction Electrocardiogram (ECG) measurements revealed that instead of a steady repeatable rhythm there was a choppy or continually variable rhythm that was detectable when located on the disturbed zone. The difference was correlated to the 95th percentile certainty. The ECG normalized after leaving the Disturbed Zone.

Coordinative Vegetative Rhythm operates in balanced coordinated rhythms, especially when at rest. Analysis showed that the pulse-breath quotient remained in balance on the Neutral Zone but was significantly uncoordinated on the Disturbed Zone.

Serotonin is diminished on the Disturbed Zone and its metabolism advanced the tendency for increased tryptophan, which is a compensating process. Serotonin is a neurotransmitter in the parasympathetic system which controls energy. This reaction was highly significant.

Investigations comparing the blood corpuscle decline speed on the Neutral Zone and the Disturbed Zone yielded significantly different behavior in 452 double-blind investigations. Blood sedimentation speed slowed in subjects on the Disturbed Zone.

Study's Conclusions

Disturbed zones should be viewed as a risk factor that can reinforce pathogenic forces. Geopathic stress on biological systems belong with risk factors such as: alcohol, environmental chemicals and pollutants, malnutrition, drugs, psycho-social stresses, genetic disposition, and electromagnetic effects.

Although this study was done in Europe, "disturbed zones" or zones of geopathic stress relating to underground water, Hartmann lines, and geological faults impact our whole planet, the United States included.

Each individual's bioelectrical system, immune system, and mental-emotional constitution are different. A person with a healthy lifestyle living or working in geopathic stress zones may experience minor influences. Another person with a mediocre and/or stressful health style may experience major influences. The literature of geopathic stress indicates effects are cumulative over time, ranging from a few to many years. Long-term exposure may aggravate predisposition to chronic or degenerative diseases.

Changing your living space into a life-supporting "conditioned space."

A method developed by Dr Hartmann in Europe and updated by Slim Spurling and geobiologists in the US detects and maps the lines and zones of geopathic stress on a property. Hartmann grid line intersections create eddy currents resulting in a counter-clockwise spin, which has been found to be detrimental to healthy biological processes. Solutions involve placing rods and other devices into the ground to neutralize the discordant energy in living and working spaces.

The solution has evolved based on research into geometric structures that resonate with the Earth's underlying gravity waves. Its simplicity is deceivingly simple. Rigid rods of specific dimensions are installed vertically in a geometric configuration that negates the geopathic stress zones. The result is a coherence of underlying standing gravity waves that are fundamental forces that influence our bio-energetic fields and the Earth's magnetic and electrical fields. This revised technique has worked successfully in over a thousand home and business applications from 2001 to the present. However, there is much more we can do to "enhance" our energetic living environments. This involves working with the fundamental force of gravity to restore energetic harmony and coherence. Or to establish a creative conditioned space, where well-being is supported and individuals can apply techniques to achieve transcendent objectives.

The evolution in understanding what gravity really is and renewed interest in an energy medium called the Aether, a common term used to describe the fundamental energy of the universe, give us information to enhance our living spaces. This leads us to develop devices resulting in a phenomenon termed gravitational coherence. Imagine one hundred people in a small room, each talking randomly about different topics in one hundred languages in different tones and pitches. You would most likely hear this as discordant noise and want to leave the room. Now imagine one hundred people singing a great symphonic chorus in one language, all in tune. You would hear a coherent harmonious succession of melodies and enjoy the sound and feelings it stirs within you. This analogy describes the application of gravitational coherence.

Gravitational coherence is a phenomenon exhibited by devices that affect the existing geometry of subtle energy fields. These geometric subtle energy fields are standing gravity waves[5] that compose the dynamic energies associated with the toroidal and vortex geometry of atomic structures.[6,7] These devices influence local energy-space through sympathetic resonant action on the energetic geometry of all elements within the gravitational medium.

Simple devices called the gravitational mean active capacitor (Gmac) and the Terra Yantra are dynamic gravitational circuits. They influence the ubiquitous medium of gravitation to cohere and bring into harmony standing gravitational waves at discrete locations. That is, a "conditioned space"[8] or sacred space, in harmonious sympathetic resonance with living biological systems. The Gmac alternates between a "positive" and "negative" polarity of gravitational coherence and the Terra Yantra simultaneously coheres positive and negative polarity of standing gravitational waves.

Equal and simultaneous application of gravitational polarities results in an equilibrium of local standing gravitational waves. This balances the expansion or "outward" radiation of negative gravitational polarity and the compression or "inward" contraction of positive gravitational polarity. The result is the Terra Yantra,

Picture of a Gmac connected to a Harmonizer[9]

a bi-polar dynamic gravitational circuit, developed in consultation with other gravity and geopathic stress researchers. The Terra Yantra can be an install and forget tool used to create conditioned spaces that also neutralize geopathic stress. The Terra Yantra is also used in combination with the Gmac's alternating gravitational polarity settings, or other resonant geometry tools for numerous functions. A descriptive interpretation of Terra Yantra means Earth (Terra) vision (Yantra). Yantra is derived from the Sanskrit root word Yam, which means to reveal the hidden energy in all elements.

As the reader is aware, our consciousness isn't separate from the geometric gravitational or electromagnetic forces composing our environment. Thoughts influence the energetic environment. Our realities are constantly changing and evolving at the speed and intent of consciousness. To quote Dr. Gilbert, "[Geometric] forms actually have an effect on the mind; they have an effect on our energy field; they have an effect on our consciousness."[10] Likewise, our focused intentions influence subtle energetic geometries. Hence the Gmac and Terra Yantra are as much tools of our consciousness as they are dynamic gravitational circuits.

Each location on our planet is composed of numerous influences that can be in harmony or discordant. The best analogy is the harmony of a well-composed and played symphony as opposed to the disharmony of musical instruments simultaneously playing music out of tune and rhythm. The local gravitational field may be in discordance or disharmony due to many influences: planetary motion, electrical and magnetic fields, local geomagnetic field variance, natural and man-made energetic structures, the local materials and their construction geometry, and especially geopathic stress zones. The influence of human emotional and mental projections of minute energy quanta cannot be excluded from influencing the local subtle energy environment.[8] When the Gmac and Terra Yantra are applied, the result is a reduction and nullification of discordant interference patterns in the local gravitational field. (This is sometimes referred to as a scalar field or scalar field potentials.[11]) A conditioned or harmonious space results, in which our activities, be they healing, working, or meditating can be far more effective.

Subjective testing and reports indicate that Gmac and Terra Yantra configurations used alone or with other advanced active geometries[8] expand the influence of gravitational coherence to create a "conditioned space." Individuals report greater emotional calm and mental clarity. As an example, one medical center in Albuquerque, NM, has cleared the geopathic stress and applies the Gmac's alternating gravitational polarity in 12 minute cycles[12] to reduce emotional and physical stress of clients. It's interesting to note that dental patients feel "very well and calm" in this facility during and after procedures.

Interviews with the owners of this medical center and other facilities demonstrate that patients are more at ease, healing protocols are conducted with far less stress, and practitioners require less time for some protocols. A Naturopathic Doctor (ND) uses applied kinesiology and other biofeedback tests to diagnose appropriate herbal and homeopathic remedies. Upon moving to a new business location, one ND had the geopathic stress neutralization procedure conducted and installed the Gmac in the new facility. The ND reported improved effectiveness of kinesiology and biofeedback in diagnosis and determining the appropriate remedies for her clients. This conditioned space has been observed by more than one hundred participants who have applied the Gmac and Terra Yantra in their living and working environments. They have reported that conditioned spaces support healing modalities, meditative and personal growth activities, and the evolution of personal consciousness. The design of scientific instrumentation is ongoing to collect hard technical data to verify individual observations.

Why do these technologies work, and how do our minds and physical bodies interact with these gravitational fields? Measurements using bioelectrical detection systems on the physical body have not shown direct electrical or magnetic field influence. Scientists hypothesize that subtle changes in the local gravitational field creates a energetically zero-stress environment in which biological and mental functions can conduct restorative activity associated with healing mechanisms and creative intention.

Our consciousness is not separate from any creation in the universe, be it a rock, a galaxy, or any being. The ubiquitous medium of gravity may be synonymous with consciousness. Call it divine spiritual energy, the Holy Spirit, the breath of Brahma, the forces of quantum interactions, or other philosophies, scientific theories, or religions. Regardless of what term, it is the medium or space-time-energy that we are a part of, and live within. Individual thoughts and emotions are part of the universal living field, the underlying creative energy of form and substance. For convenience, call it the creative Aether.

Manifestation is a direct result of thoughts and emotions holding an image or pattern, projected into this Aether. If the manifesting "desire" is clear and operates in a coherent non-chaotic energetic environment, then it can "mold" the underlying creative energy of form and substance into manifestation. The Gmac and Terra Yantra, and other devices like them are tools in this living time and space to shape form and substance.

The clearing of geopathic stress and use of the Gmac and Terra Yantra or other similar devices do not add or inject any new energy into our living space-time. They restore the natural harmony and coherent resonance to that underlying creative energy or Aether, the raw material of creation.

In short, this creates a conditioned space-energy, in the now moment, that results in a manifestation in form and substance. Within these conditioned spaces the universe and its creative energy rearranges itself to meet our vision of reality. The old saying is appropriate, "be careful what you ask for, you might get it"!

About Peter Jackson

Peter Jackson has been researching and developing technologies and products to neutralize geopathic stress and improve living and working spaces for over twenty years. His expertise includes geophysics, systems engineering, dowsing, alternative healing modalities, and the creation and testing of advanced traditional as well as alternative technologies. He teaches beginning and advanced workshops in understanding and neutralizing geopathic influences on physical and mental well-being. In his workshops he teaches "hands-on" application of the Gmac and Terra Yantra technologies along with other related products and techniques to create harmonious living and working environments. Peter consults with other professionals in the healing arts and sciences, and conducts technical reviews of geopathic stress reduction products.

He currently lives and works in New Mexico, and can be reached at pjackson64@comcast.com.

On the Other Side

I put all of my conditioning aside
for one glorious instant and slide
through the eye of the needle,
threading it with light. On the
other side there is no portal
for return, but I don't even
think about that. Cutting the
cord, I dance as I never dared in
that other world, dance as if I
am loosed from gravity and
delivered into the arms of
jubilation. Reveling, merging,
spiraling inward or out, down
or up, alive and wild, I am
freed even from what I believed
freedom would be.

Danna Faulds, *From Root to Bloom*

CHAPTER 7

A Funny Thing Happened on the Way to Ascension

Dian A. Marincola

The road to Ascension has been an action-packed adventure so far. There has been so much to see and do. I've had a few setbacks on the way and some of the activities have been a bit scary, but I've learned so much. I've increased my vocabulary, made light-minded friends, and gained a whole new perspective on perspective. I have a deeper understanding of pop culture, found a new respect for the entertainment industry, learned how *not* to tell time, and found out that God and I come from the same home town. And to think that just a few short years ago, Ascension was something that others did. Who knew!

To be honest, I had stopped thinking about the Ascension several decades ago when I switched from parochial to public school and no longer got the day off. My memory was fuzzy but I was sure that I was supposed to be dead when Ascension happened. I was still alive. How could I rise from the dead without being dead? Wasn't it supposed to happen on Judgment Day? And isn't Judgment Day the day that I died? Am I going to die in 2012 just because the Mayan calendar ends then? What do they mean by the end of time? What is Ascension anyway?

Having been raised a Roman Catholic, the term Ascension had always meant that Jesus Christ rose up to heaven under his own power, 40 days after his resurrection from the dead, on Easter Sunday. (It happened on a Thursday.) Catholics believe that Christ's Ascension is the promise of their own ascension into heaven. According to church doctrine, the Ascension is "the final elevation of Christ's human nature into the condition of divine glory."[1] It is the ultimate work of redemption, the salvation of humanity by Jesus Christ.

Over the past few years, I have managed to broaden my understanding of Ascension to include concepts from other belief systems and traditions that take a more cosmic perspective:

- expansion of consciousness
- clearing limiting beliefs and clarifying inner focus
- being at one with the Higher Self and the Soul

- transformation of the planet Earth and the human population

The first three bullet points are more related to personal Ascension, yet are interconnected to the fourth bullet point, Planetary Ascension.

Today, I am in more of a "here and now" rather than "later" mode of Ascension. My path to Ascension does not have much of a strategy, nor do I believe one is necessary. One of my favorite games as a child was "Chutes and Ladders," an uncomplicated game of rewards and consequences. To play, you go with the flow as determined by a spin of a dial. My path is similar to playing the game. My physical, emotional, mental, and spiritual bodies all get to play. I can see this cosmic game board neatly laid out before me. The rules are so simple. There is no predetermined path to end the game. Each spin of the dial presents a new lesson to learn in my desire to move forward. If I learn the lesson I move forward and land squarely in a block; occasionally, my consciousness takes a jump and I get to climb the ladder and move up much higher in vibration. Next spin, I may land on a square and have to slide down a chute because I really did not learn the life lesson well enough to practice it and sustain the higher vibration. I spin again and I move forward. In the end, I reach the last square of the track. Game over. Time to move on.

Every spot that I have landed on in the cosmic game board has offered new insights, challenges, gifts, and rewards. Thus far I am having an extraordinary adventure…

"Change is inevitable; growth is optional." Walt Disney

If my cats Pywacket and Dixie had gotten along better, I may not have gotten out the game board and made my first move towards simply Being. For years, I had led a very quiet and rather uninspired life. Me, myself, and I were living alone together rather comfortably in a small duplex within the Washington-Annapolis-Baltimore corridor. Late one summer, two small fur balls took up residence with me. One might say that they were my wake-up call. As you may have learned, the universe will get your attention, one way or another.

Pywacket had staked her claim in our home one month before Dixie, a stray that friends found, moved in. As the alpha, Pye was not happy to have another cat sharing her space. Pye would attack Dixie at random and without provocation. It started off with Pye batting Dixie in the head. This was followed by a chase sequence that ended only when Dixie had successfully jumped up onto the kitchen counter, then to the top of the refrigerator, finally ending with one last jump onto the top of the cabinets. Safely snuggled, Dixie would spend hours up in her roost, away from Pye's menacing demeanor. Every day: bat, chase, jump, jump, jump. It drove me crazy.

Not wanting to tranquilize Pye as I knew my vet would recommend, I took my friend Kate's suggestion and took my girls to see an animal communicator named Gina.

After a brief conversation with each, Gina told me what was troubling Pye and what was on Dixie's mind. Due to their right to privacy, I won't go into the details. Suffice it to say that *my* behavior needed modification if peace were to return to our humble abode. Before I took the girls home to begin anew, Gina gave me a puzzled look and asked if we had met before. I said "No." Next, Gina raised her hand for a few seconds above what I now know to be my heart chakra and said, "Oh, you are Reiki, so am I."

If you are unfamiliar with Reiki, it may be defined as a form of energy medicine that originated by Dr. Mikao Usui in Japan in the mid-1880s. Simply stated, Reiki practitioners believe that disturbances in the flow of energy in the physical, mental, emotional, and spiritual fields cause dis-ease. We seek to improve the flow and balance of energy to heal.

I did take Gina's advice and found a Reiki Master near my home and began the attunements and training a few months later. Funny how you meet people who direct you to a place that you would have missed if left to your own map reading abilities. Synchronicity, and our ability to recognize and respond to it, are described in James Redfield's *The Celestine Prophecy*[2] as The Seventh Insight, Engaging the Flow. Kate pointed me to Gina who pointed me to Reiki. Reiki pointed me to many light-minded friends including teachers, massage therapists, truck drivers, college students, psychologists, naturopaths, energy workers, civil servants, physical therapists, house painters, database administrators, and trees.

"You talkin to me?"

I met Henry several years ago. He called out to me quite unexpectedly while I was walking up the footpath to visit Kate and Judy, friends who at the time were living in an old Victorian house near Henry's own residence. At first, I could not figure out who was calling to me. I looked around, but didn't see anyone. It was late afternoon and the shadows were long. Suddenly, I realized that there was no clear direction for the sound of the voice. It was as if the voice was coming from speakers inside my head. I surveyed the yard again until I focused in on a great pin oak tree on the side of the house. With that, the voice sounded again, "Hello!" After the theme from "The Twilight Zone" stopped playing in my head, I mumbled something inspired like, "May I help you?" If animals can communicate, I thought, why not trees?

Henry introduced himself and asked me to come to where he was standing so that we could chat a bit. He didn't like shouting across the yard even if his voice could only be heard inside my head. He thought it rude. I hesitated at first because he was standing in the part of the yard that I knew would be swarming with mosquitoes during that time of day. Hearing my thoughts, Henry assured me that if I came closer, the mosquitoes would not bother me. I did and they didn't.

Very old, tall, and stately, Henry had a simple request. He was lonely and missed the parties that former occupants of the house had often hosted during his youth. He showed me glimpses of those parties in that part of the brain that project onto the inner eye. He asked me to intervene on his behalf and make sure that there was music. He really liked music. It never occurred to me to ask Henry why he didn't ask them himself.

Walking up the steps to my friends' front door, I wasn't sure how to ask them to throw a party for the tree in their yard. By nature I am not comfortable in unfamiliar social situations. So, as I climbed the steps, I practiced in my head what I was going to say. Maybe someone else was in there and could offer some advice.

"Hey, I just spoke to your pin oak, and he wants you to throw a party!" Nah, a bit too forward.

How about, "I just met Henry and he wants you to host a party for him."

"Who's Henry?"

"Henry is that big oak tree in your yard."

"No, I am not under a lot of stress at work."

Nah, that won't work, either.

Hmmm...I could start off with "Boy, that Henry is quite a talker!" But, that would just circle back to "Who's Henry?"

So, I started off the conversation with the standard introductory line, "You're not going to believe what just happened..." But Kate and Judy did believe me. Within a few weeks, they had a great party for Henry, complete with kids, music, and lots of love.

"Seek not to change the world, but choose to change your mind about the world."[3] - *A Course In Miracles*

Trees are amazing creations. Give one a hug sometime and you will experience a wonderful sensation. Long before I met Henry, I was told to go hug a tree because I was having trouble getting grounded after a group meditation. New to both meditation and the people in the group, I wasn't sure if they were serious. If nothing else, the walk to the trees would help clear my head. And, if I heard any giggling from the group, I could just keep on walking into the sunset. Feeling silly, but still drowsy I wrapped my arms around the trunk of a small tree and leaned in to snuggle. What an extraordinary feeling!

With my ear firmly against the trunk I could hear these vibrant undulating sounds. I was told later by the woman leading the meditation that trees help bring energy down from the universe into the earth through their crowns where it is transmitted from their trunks into their roots. Their root systems span for miles and miles both across and down into the earth's crust. This is why trees are so good at helping humans ground themselves. Their long and complex root systems also form a sophisticated communication network from tree to tree to tree. As long as their roots touch, they can send and receive information from one another across a wide expanse.

Their fibrous trunks are data stores of information collected from both their leaves and their roots. Consequently, trees have very good memories of our material world.

***"You know that we are living in a material world. And I am a material girl"*[4]** Madonna

So what exactly is a material world? Exploring this concept has been the most mind-boggling for me. There are so many perspectives and disciplines, each saying the same thing, but using different terminology. I've yet to find my universal translator or Rosetta Stone.

Simply put, the material world is our plane of existence, a dimension of dense matter where we, as spiritual beings, can have the human experience. During Ascension, we seek to rise above the limitations of our material world by increasing our vibration to enter the next dimension.

In keeping with my game board analogy, the material or physical world is the playground for us to play at being human. It is an amazing place. We get to shape, mold, bend, and create our own reality. Did I mention that cosmic Chutes and Ladders is interactive?

Some teachings refer to our material world as the paradoxical world of illusion,[5] or separation from spirit. It is based on the supposition that if you believe everything you experience through your five senses is real, then God is an illusion. If God is real, then everything you experience through your five senses is an illusion. We live life (as an illusion) so that we can awaken to our God Self as reality or Truth. Therein lies the paradox.

I have a feeling I won't be spinning the dial anytime soon as I try to figure this one out!

Earth plays an important role in the human experience. If you think about it, without the Earth we couldn't have a human experience.

I recall vividly the first time I met the Earth Spirit. She showed up at a healing circle a group of us were having for her several years ago. Well, "meet" may be too strong a word. I didn't actually talk to her then. But she stood about five feet from where I was standing. She was dressed all in wispy golden white threads that night and was having an intimate conversation with the person who was to lead the meditation. Somehow, she reminded me of Glinda the Good Witch from *The Wizard of Oz*. "There's no place like home. There's no place like home."

In researching Hawaiian spiritual practices I learned that the Earth plays an important role for the Ascendant. Remember when I mentioned earlier that tree hugging is a great way to get grounded? "Essentially, being grounded means being IN your body, conscious of your surroundings and present and available for whatever happens."[6] If you are not in your body, you cannot transcend the limitations of the physical plane and ascend. This was an "Ah Ha" moment for me! Suddenly things started coming together for me. Now, I just need to figure out illusion and reality.

Another aspect of the material world is that it is governed by specific laws. Perhaps, the most well-known of them is the Law of Attraction.

Law of Attraction – Where attention goes; energy flows

The Law of Attraction has gained renewed exposure in the mass market due to the works of Michael Losier, Esther and Jerry Hicks, Rhonda Byrne, and others. I first became aware of this powerful law by reading Catherine Ponder's work, *The Dynamic Laws of Prosperity*,[7] during the early stages of my road trip. This book has been my trusted travel companion ever since.

The Law of Attraction is one of the easiest to remember: "like attracts like." Whatever you think about you bring into your life, whether you wanted it or not.

Therein lies the conundrum. You have to have a clear understanding of your beliefs and let go of old thought forms to achieve the life you desire.

It's a lot of work! It is like peeling away the layers of an onion that won the "Prize for Greatest Girth" at the state fair. Peel back one layer only to find that there is some other thought form that you have to re-evaluate. Belief systems are hierarchical in structure. I've been trying to get to the core of my plantar fasciitis for over a year. In the meantime, I've experienced some kind of fracture in my left foot, which is the foot where the condition started. Now my right foot is bothering me. Whatever this issue is wants to be resolved or reconciled before I can move forward.

Now, you are probably thinking, "Why don't you look it up in Louise Hay (referring to the handy pocket book *Heal Your Body*[8]) and see what she says?" I did. Louise pointed me in a direction, but I still have to do the work. Knowing the cause and saying the affirmation, without restructuring my beliefs, doesn't work.

With intent, I have tried to use the Law of Attraction to manifest my desires. By virtue of the law itself, I am very successful . . . at reminding myself of the old adage "Be careful what you wish for." The intentional process for attracting what you want to bring into your life is simple, but not easy:

- State clearly what you want and focus on it.
- Affirm it. Visualize it. Work at it.
- Be grateful.
- Allow it.

I have great difficulty in figuring out what I want so I get stalled at step one. Then, I formulate these "this or that" statements. "If I can't have this, then how about that?" I actually work hard at visualizing all of these scenarios and affirming them. I say "Thank you, Universe." "Manifest quickly, Universe, according to your own good plan." "Wait a minute; is it too late to change my order? Instead of...." Hey, what was I thinking, this is all an illusion!

There are other universal laws that govern our material world as told in Dan Millman's parable *The Laws of Spirit: A Tale of Transformation*.[9] Millman's tale identifies 12 laws, including the Laws of Presence, Compassion, Cycles, Balance, and Unity.

Since then I have learned of other laws worth mentioning for which, unfortunately, no serious books have been written.

The Law of Exhaustion

This law states that as our energetic bodies spin faster in response to accelerated frequencies of light coming into the planet, we will struggle to sleep at night. When we finally do get to sleep, we will awaken between the hours of 2:00 a.m. and 4:00 a.m. We will be very tired during the day.

The Law of Weird

This law postulates that the definition of what we deem weird will change as new gifts and talents present themselves, as we become exposed to the gifts and talents of others, as we expand our consciousness into other dimensions, and as we learn other universal laws. Examples of terms, concepts, or practices that have transitioned from being considered weird include astral projection, aura reading, animal communication, acupuncture, energy blocks, subjective reality, energy medicine, light worker, channeling, Merkaba, past life regression, and Ascension. Unfortunately, talking to trees is still considered as weird in many circles. However, talking to plants is not.

The Law of Workshops

This law states that the universe will offer a workshop on any technique or concept that was introduced by the Law of the Weird.

The Law of Why Did You?

This law states that as you seek sympathy from your light-minded friends regarding some new illness or painful situation that you are suffering, their first response will be "Why did you bring that into your life?"

The Law of What The…?

This laws says that as we seek mastery to achieve the life we desire through the Law of Attraction, we will be presented with many outcomes for which our initial response will be, "What the?" What the? may also describe my egoic thoughts regarding Planetary Ascension.

"It is not the strongest of the species that survive, nor the most intelligent, but the one that proves itself the most responsive to change." Charles Darwin

Perhaps the most frequent depiction of Planetary Ascension in popular culture is the cartoon where a long-haired bearded guy is wearing a white robe and carrying a sign that says, "The End is Near."

So what is the End? Apocalyptic passages of the Bible as well as ancient texts of the Mayans, Sumer, Egypt and Vedic literatures of India regard it as the end of time. It could be the moment when humanity, Planet Earth, the Milky Way Galaxy and perhaps all of known creation takes a synchronized leap in evolution. Only time will tell.

And when is the End? Wisdom teachings say sometime towards the end of 2012. Opinions vary. My own opinion is that it ends when I reach the last square in my game of cosmic "Chutes and Ladders."

About Dian A. Marincola

Dian A. Marincola is a Certified *Traditional Usui Reiki and Karuna Reiki™ Master Teacher* living in the Metropolitan Washington, DC – Baltimore area.

CHAPTER 8

AWAKE – A Sufi Ascension Practice

Ramana Smallen

Over the centuries, there have always been those who are called mystics, who have become well acquainted with the inner landscapes. It has been said that it was easier in earlier times for the mystical attunement, and more commonplace. The industrial age and modern ways have been blamed for this more superficial and attractive lifestyle, especially in the west. This serves to bring our attention to a more mundane level.

My teacher, Pir Vilayat Khan, a Sufi Master, who passed in 2002, used to say that we find ourselves stuck in the "middle ranges." He was fond of saying "AWAKE!" He asked us to imagine we were a visitor from another galaxy, brought to the planet to observe conditions down here, to report back. We would feel the pull of gravity on our bodies and minds, and the sense of limitation and isolation inherent in this point of view. We were to somehow compress our beings to this compartmentalized condition, so we might be more accurate in our portrayal of the point of view of our co-inhabitants. This, of course, was a metaphor for what he knew to be the real situation. We seek a way to escape the gravity, or glue, which keeps us tied down.

The Sufis say, "I am in the world but not of the world." Rumi says, "Harken to the wail of the reed who has been cut from the reed bed" (referring to the Ney, which is a flute that sounds like what the soul might call out in longing for re-union).

Although the term ascension is not commonly used among my companions, the idea and the practice is. We, who take initiation in the Sufi Order International, are stepping upon a path to the unknown. We know it is a spiritual training that is customized to our individual needs. We know that this training will include the opportunity to step beyond our comfort zone. But we do not know what that will feel like, or what words to use to describe it. Indeed, we quickly discover that if we can describe it, it is not so real. We find that we have not yet hit the "mark."

I used the word awake. What can we say about it? The Sufi says, "The Message is a call to those whose hour has come to awake and it is a lullaby for those who are still meant to sleep."[1] It also says that it is a sin to awaken someone before their time. In fact, I wonder whether it is possible. The mind will always try to find some way to wrap itself around an experience it can't comprehend. You might call it resistance.

I just returned from a long retreat during which I was alone, in the woods, except for the once-a-day visit from the guide. I have noticed that each retreat is different. Things emerge in their own time. This time I watched as the layers were removed, day by day. I saw that I was getting closer to layers that had never before been touched before in my being. This was a healing retreat, where the practices that were employed were guided by the stuff that presented itself, rather than an attempt to lift through certain alchemical levels, regardless of what emerged.

In this case, the layers were consisting of stuff that my "little boy" had saved me from as a child, and was still holding on to in an effort to continually protect me. Part of this process is a sort of update, to show that little boy who I am now, that those scary things are no longer life and death, but excess baggage that might now be opened, looked at, and released. It was like gaining access to doorways into rooms that were previously off limits. We all have little boys or girls who are busy putting things away, or helping us forget those scary movies.

Having released some of this baggage has afforded me an opportunity to experience things with more depth and space. When a new car comes on the market, it is sold with a certain horsepower engine. This is a limit within the design. In order to get more horsepower, you need a new engine with a different design. I feel that I have more horsepower, but that I somehow did not need a new design. It is still me, but there is a better spiritual engine. Perhaps I am more aware of essential flow within and through me.

Back to AWAKE.

One day I had an answer to a question that had been hanging around so long I forgot it was there…until the answer. The question: Is the soul perfect? The background to the question is found in the prayer we often say in the Sufi Healing Order.

>Nayaz
>
>Beloved Lord, almighty God.
>
>Through the rays of the sun.
>
>Through the waves of the air.
>
>Through the all pervading life in space.
>
>Purify, and revivify me, and I pray.
>
>Heal my body, heart and soul.
>
>Amin

So, if the soul is perfect, why does it need healing? That is what was hanging around. The answer came in the form of a class on the soul that my guide was leading. In this class we were reading from works on Hazrat Inayat Khan, Pir Vilayat's father and predecessor, the founder of the Sufi Movement, and the author of the Sufi Message. To paraphrase: The soul is perfect. Not subject to birth, death, and illness as we who inhabit our bodies are. The soul is a condition of the spirit, not separate from it. It is perfectly impressionable, however. Otherwise, what would animate us? What would look out through the eyes? The soul thinks it is us, or what is before it. It thinks it has the qualities, or lack of qualities before it. It thinks it is ill or weak, if we think that. It thinks it is stuck in the body if we think that. It is subject to doubts and fears if we are. It thinks its outlook is limited to what is before it.

It is in our capacity to free the soul from this suffering. To awake from the slumber we force upon the soul by inhabiting the middle ranges. With a shift in our identity, we might soften the hold we have on our personality. We could let in some air between the spaces; to take ourselves less seriously. Perhaps, to ascend. And, thus we try to give expression to the needs and emotions of the soul.

The ancient Sufis did practices to address this issue. They called it *Fana`* or annihilation. Another meaning for this term is "going through." We are passing through from the limited view to the true realization. The approach is to shatter our being on the rock of truth…in stages. We first annihilate ourselves in the being of our teacher, who is our first example of someone who has worked with this which is known as the first stage -- *Fana Fi Sheikh*. In my case, I found myself copying the mannerisms of my guide, and dropping my own. This, of course, was merely a shadow of the practice. The advanced practice within this stage is *Baqa,* where you enter into the consciousness of the teacher.

As this works to open your horizons, you eventually reach the next stage: *Fana Fi Rasoul* or annihilation in the prophet; the teacher of the teacher. I experience this as a great expansion of being, coupled with profound purpose. The path of the prophet is the utmost in the challenge to humanity: to be human and experience the limits inherent thereof and simultaneously to be the Herald of the Divine Being. One can reach to the stage where one says "I am the eyes through which God sees!" I am not referring to the need to bring forth a new religion, but to enter into the consciousness of one who might inspire that impulse. This takes time. It requires shattering of one's assumptions, point of view, sense of identity, and aspiration.

The next stage is *Fana Fi Allah* or shattering in the consciousness of the Divine Being. It is at this stage where poetry often is needed since words are so limiting, and one must otherwise descend in order to convey some part of the depth, meaning, breadth, moment, vastness, boundlessness. The *Baqa* of *Fana Fi Allah* is a very intimate examination of one's identity as divine. One needs to let go of the last vestiges of separation. One no longer looks up for God. The dichotomies which have caused suffering are past.

> *"You are my life; it is in you that I live,*
>
> *From you I borrow life and you do I give;*
>
> *O my soul and spirit, you I adore,*
>
> *I live in you, so do I live evermore.*
>
> *You are in me, and in you do I live,*
>
> *Still you are my King and my sins you forgive,*
>
> *You are the present and Future and Past;*
>
> *I lost myself, but I have found you at last."*[2]
>
> Hazrat Inayat Khan

How are *Fana* and *Baqa* approached? They are approached with intention, love, devotion, dedication, grace and with a guide. The Sufi refers to *Maqam* and *Hal* as a way to discuss this process. *Maqam* is your station. Think of this as your outlook, or the way you view the world in which you find yourself. This includes your occupation, your relationships, your understanding, how it feels to be you, your gestalt, what you see about your purpose in life, etc. You are working with what has been given to you from within and without at this station. You might see this as working your way up a small hill, with some advancement when there is a small breakthrough in realization, and perhaps a setback or two in moments of confusion or frustration, or anxiety. But eventually you get clearly up the small hill, where you may look to the next valley, and the following hill. These may be seen as the next challenges and perhaps the next set of breakthroughs or realizations to come. You proceed by doing the inner and outer work you were doing on the last station, but it has perhaps a different theme, or level of difficulty, or there is more at stake, etc. This may be seen as the way the waves of progress on the spiritual path might be mapped. Every map is different.

Then there is the *Hal*. We attribute this to grace, since there appears to be no other reason for it. You are somehow raised above your station. You are raised to a point where you may see many stations ahead and behind. Your view of the world has new depth, height, breadth. You see purpose where you saw challenge and mystery before. It is like peeking behind the veil. Pir Vilayat would say: "Can you see that which transpires behind that which appears?" This state is often associated with great affirmation or ecstasy. The great teachers are said to be able to pick the person in this state out of the crowd.

This process includes several stages of revelation, followed by lots of inner work that brings you toward the next level of realization. This is how the mystic is born. He or she may begin to be called a seer. One of the hallmarks of the seer is the facility of taking almost any point of view. The seer discovers that the dichotomies he or she is aware of, and takes a position on, are comfortably encompassed by the vastness found within. Rich-poor, high-low, right-wrong, large-small, birth-death, etc. Integration is found when you can hold both sides, rather than get stuck on the continuum somewhere. The partisan who says that God is on **my** side, leaves out that God is also on the other's side, and that the real **side** is in remembrance. This is another way of saying that the life drama you have just been through has its roots in the Divine Being, and is really pointing to, or hinting at the source, which is the Divine Being.

The guide's purpose is to look at the soul of the one before it and see what is emerging, what is in need of encouraging, and to give practices that might give expression to what is in the wings. Many times, this is in the form of a sacred phrase, or the repetition of a Divine Quality. Ancient, sacred language is often employed for this, such as Arabic as it carries the historical weight of the collective unconscious, and it invokes the science of sound as it may influence our experience, or capacity. The effect of sound is employed with the use of name change. When a student is ready, he or she may request a new name from the guide, who is expected to be intuitive enough to hear that name come through.

When your spiritually oriented friends call you by that name, it has an effect. There is something powerful about having a taken name, rather than a given name (from your birth parents). In my case, it opened me to a part of my spiritual inheritance that was previously hidden.

Besides sound, one may work with breath. Several basic breath practices are employed that may help one in balance and purification. It is perhaps surprising to discover the power in breath, as we have usually taken it for granted most of our life, or think of it in terms of the exchange of gases which then feed the cells, and remove waste. There is so much more offered in working with the breath. Experience the Element Purification practice and see for yourself.

Element Purification Practice

Breath: We are made of elements. I am referring to the elements of the ancients, not the elemental chart of science. They are Earth, Water, Fire, Air and Ether. In this practice we will attune to each of these units in our makeup, in turn.

Earth: Breathe in through the nose and exhale from the nose, naturally. As you do this, be aware of energy coming in from the base of the spine and rising up, past each of the chakras. You are bringing in energy or magnetism from the earth, which is ready to be your supplier of fresh energy. On the out breath, feel the polluted energy descend, and return to Earth for recycling. Each breath gives you an opportunity to make room for fresh energy, and you gradually feel lighter, and clearer. On the third breath, begin to feel some extra energy, which might be shared with the world through the heart center as you breathe out. Not only will polluted energy continue to descend, but some of the excess fresh energy is radiated out from the heart as a beacon. You are aware of the horizon spreading before you, and the subtle qualities of energized Amber come to mind.

Water: Breathe in through the nose and exhale from the mouth. This breath is attuned to that which flows within and without your being. There is a further purification, as though you are in a shower. The in breath brings a rise in the water level, and the out breath unleashes the water energy to enhance flow, and carry away more of this waste. There is a sense of downward flow, and one may find the color green is emerging. There may also be a sense of the flow of Divine Qualities as they surface in you.

Fire: Breathe in through the mouth and exhale from the nose. You have a temperature from the constant combustion process physically inside you; there is also a sense of combustion associated with the burning of impurities. On the in breath, you feel the flames growing inside as the "still small flame within" burns brighter. When you feel those flames reach the heart center, it is a transition point where the heart transmutes that fire into light. You burn intensely, and glow intensely from inside. As this continues, you may find the part of you that was always a being of light. It is sometimes hard to find, because everyone around you is also burning brightly. The difference is that you are aware of it.

This discovery is the beginning of a chapter of life where you are in communication with other beings of light in other realms, leading to discovery of your being beyond the light that is visible and definable. But for now, it is enough that you feel further purified by this breath.

Air: Breathe in through the mouth and exhale from the mouth. As you breathe in, you are filled with a lofty sense of being everywhere at once. As you breathe out, you are dismantled and disseminated throughout the universe. There is no single direction to your travels. It is going where you are drawn, whenever you are drawn there. There is nothing really left of you as a solid, contained being. The impurities you were working with before are so slight now as to be imperceptible. As the breeze blows, it blows through you. You are aware, on the atomic level, of the great spaces between the particles of matter that make you visible.

Ether: Breathe in and out from the mouth and nose - very subtle and refined breath. This is the source of the elements, and very little is needed for the creation of your separate being. Just a few breaths here, and the practice ends. If you stay in this breath too long, you might be caught in the mist.

This practice ends with a wish that as you have opened yourself thus, you might enjoy the freedom and balance and lightness, and that healing in all levels of your being might occur. Repeat the prayer on page 124 (Nayaz).

Those of us in the Sufi world often take this as a daily practice.

"The ideal perfection, called Baqa by Sufis, is termed 'Najat' in Islam, 'Nirvana' in Buddhism, 'Salvation' in Christianity, and 'Mukhti' in Hinduism. This is the highest condition attainable, and all ancient prophets and sages experienced it, and taught it to the world.

Baqa is the original state of God. At this state every being must arrive some day, consciously or unconsciously, before or after death. The beginning and end of all beings is the same, the difference only existing during the journey.

There are three ways in man's journey towards God. The first is the way of ignorance, through which each must travel. It is like a person walking for miles in the sun while carrying a heavy load on his shoulder, who, when fatigued, throws away the load and falls asleep under the shade of a tree. Such is the condition of the average person, who spends his life blindly under the influence of his senses and gathers the load of his evil actions; the agonies of his earthly longings creating a hell through which he must pass to reach the destination of his journey. With regard to him the Qur'an says, 'He who is blind in life, shall also be blind in the hereafter.'

The next way is that of devotion, which is for true lovers. Rumi says, 'Man may be the lover of man or the lover of God; after his perfection in either he is taken before the King of love.' Devotion is the heavenly wine, which intoxicates the devotee until his heart becomes purified from all infirmities and there remains the happy vision of the Beloved, which lasts to the end of the journey. 'Death is a bridge, which unites friend to friend' (Sayings of Mohammed).

The third is the way of wisdom, accomplished only by the few. The disciple disregards life's momentary comforts, unties himself from all earthly bondages and turns his eyes toward God, inspired with divine wisdom. He gains command over his body, his thoughts and feelings, and is thereby enabled to create his own heaven within himself, that he may rejoice until merged into the eternal goal. 'We have stripped the veil from thine eyes, and thy sight today is keen', says the Qur'an. All must journey along one of these three paths, but in the end they arrive at one and the same goal. As it is said in the Qur'an, 'It is He who multiplied you on the earth, and to Him you shall be gathered.'"[3]

Hazrat Inayat Khan

About Ramana Smallen

Ramana Smallen is a long time student of Sufism. He is a senior teacher in the Sufi Order International, and a Shafayat (teacher) in the Sufi Healing Order. He has a center for Sufi Studies called the

Ishk (love) Center in Silver Spring Md. His current inspiration is exploration of new ways to work with breath and consciousness, particularly with healing. He can be reached at ramana3@verizon.net.

Let It Go

Let go of the way you thought life would unfold; the holding of plans or dreams or expectations – Let it all go. Save your strength to swim with the tide. The choice to fight what is here before you now will only result in struggle, fear and desperate attempts to flee from the very energy you long for. Let go. Let it all go and flow with the grace that washes through your days whether you receive it gently or with all your quills raised to defend against invaders. Take this on faith: the mind may never find the explanations that it seeks, but you will move forward nonetheless. Let go, and the wave's crest will carry you to unknown shores, beyond your wildest dreams or destinations. Let it all go and find the place of rest and peace and certain transformation.

Danna Faulds, *Go In and In*

CHAPTER 9

Releasing Attachments

Linda Brent

"Every day in life something is acquired, every day in the Tao, something is released." *Lao Tzu, 2500, BC.*

The above quotation by Lao Tzu simplifies the process of releasing our attachments and arriving at a compassionate, all knowing place. The process of releasing our attachments allows us to become an expression of our authentic nature. In doing so, we ascend to higher levels of knowing and experiencing ourselves and others.

Let us begin by taking a look at our overall belief system regarding materialistic attachments. In our society, there is a belief that not only should we accumulate "stuff" but the more "stuff" we have, the better. We think that having the right "stuff" actually grants us a certain degree of status and acceptance from our peers. In reality, this could not be farther from the truth. Living to compete, contend, or appease others is very limiting, very stressful, and eventually it will take its toll on our health and well-being. Most often, people who exist to live up to the expectations of others find themselves depressed, facing large amounts of debt, and/or with lots of emotional, mental and physical clutter blocking their way to a happy, healthy lifestyle.

That said, there is nothing wrong with being comfortable, having a nice home, a dependable vehicle, nice clothes and fun toys, as long as we maintain balance and proper motivation, and stay within our means. In fact, it is part of our birthright to have abundance in every way! The key is to stop and ask yourself about the motive behind the acquisitions: do you already have a lot of "stuff" that you don't even use? Are you in debt and buying more things just to have them, even though you can't afford it? Do you feel the real you is hiding behind your "stuff"? Do you fear that you won't be as popular if you don't have the latest, greatest,… everything? An important thing to keep in mind is that anything in excess is not healthy and keeps you tethered to the exterior world, which prevents you from going within to get in touch with the real you.

So…how do we create a healthy mindset with regard to acquiring new stuff? A good Feng Shui book can guide you through the principles of setting up your personal home and office space in order to support yourself energetically. In any case, you will want to begin to downsize by removing items that no longer serve you. Walk away from new purchases. If something stays with you once you've walked away and you really feel like it is yours, then go back for it. But don't let the fear of someone else getting it control you. If it is meant to be yours, it will be there when you go back, or it will come to you at a later time in your life. Giving yourself a brief pause before making a purchase is just the first step, but beginning to think in this way will start to create a healthier mindset and a more supportive energetic space.

Besides being attached to material things, we are, as a society, very attached and controlled by our relationships. Committed relationships -- whether the commitment is through birth, marriage, friendship or employment -- often create an unhealthy energetic dynamic. People tend toward feelings of ownership over other people in their lives, wanting to control what others do and how they act. Some even feel they are an authority over another person; an expert on what is right and wrong for the other person based on their own personal experiences and beliefs. This dynamic is, in truth, not at all what is right or wrong for someone else, but what is right and wrong for the person giving the advice! We really have no way of knowing what is a correct action for another person; we cannot know what lessons someone else needs to experience. All that you can really offer another is what has been helpful to you, all the while providing an unconditionally supportive space for the people in your life to experience their own consequences and learn their own lessons.

I have observed through relationships in my life that most people believe that, if a person in their life behaves in a certain way or says certain things, it will make them happy. In reality, happiness comes from within oneself. If you think about it, we are symbolically and physically released from attachments to other human beings at birth, with the cutting of the umbilical cord. Of course, there is an element of caring between people and a natural way of relating to others that creates a balanced energetic exchange and allows everyone's needs to be met. We can serve the people in our lives and achieve that balance through respect, unconditional love and acceptance. To accomplish this, we must first learn to love and accept ourselves unconditionally. As a result, our external interactions will become filled with unconditional love and acceptance of others.

We tend to judge and control others based on our own limited belief system, a belief system that was built on what our parents, church, government, employer and teachers instilled in us; this is the foundation of our conditioning. Even though we may appreciate the knowledge and perceptions of the authority figures in our life, after all, they had our best intentions at heart, right? Maybe so, but now is the time to begin questioning everything. Be careful what you hold yourself and others accountable to, you could be impeding growth and developmental opportunities for all concerned. If you are not as healthy or happy as you would like to be, then start here and reevaluate your conditioned beliefs on what is right and wrong. Even better, ponder this - is there really a right and wrong at all? Question everything…

In reality, it is enough to share our experience and knowledge to help guide others, without judgment and only when asked! Ideally, everyone should experience the opportunities and consequences of their own actions in order to grow and develop according to their individual path.

As humanity moves forward on this planet, human beings are being called to a higher, more supportive way of interaction. The only way one can truly be happy is to allow others to be expressions of their authentic selves. Only in this way can we truly know the other person; otherwise, we create a dynamic where the people in our lives are pretending to be someone they are not, doing and saying what they think we want in order to meet our expectations and needs. It is best to know and interact with the true nature of others rather than interacting with someone that is just doing and saying what they think someone wants to hear, just to meet their need. Some people will spend a very long time trying to make a relationship work instead of seeing it clearly and moving on, if necessary, to allow the right situation to enter their life.

It's now time to begin questioning everything: the way in which we choose to interact with others, our automatic responses and reactions, and any "carved in stone" belief system we may be holding regarding our attachments to people, places, and things. Only then can we begin to see that there is no one "out there," or outside of us, that can make us happy. However, as you become that which you want others to be, your outer world begins to align with your authentic self and allows the joy and sense of purpose to enter your life.

Finding the Balance

Releasing attachments and living in harmony and balance is, of course, easier said than done. However, this is an area of our lives that we cannot ignore because we are being called to interact with all beings from a more detached, non-judgmental place. As we begin to replace old thought patterns and responses with interactions that come from the unconditional love within us, things will begin to turn out better than we could ever imagine.

As Lao Tzu wrote almost 5000 years ago, "every day in the Tao, something is **released**." Try to release something everyday, whether it is mental, physical or emotional clutter. This will start to shift your expectations and perceptions of the world outside of you and begin to peel away the many layers of the onion to reveal the core of your authentic self.

About Linda Brent

Linda Brent is a Usui and Karuna Reiki™ Master and a lifelong student of Taoist teachings. She is the owner of True Relaxation Wellness Center in Centreville, MD.

True Relaxation Wellness Center

621 Railroad Ave

Centreville, Maryland 21617

410-758-0822

www.truerelaxation.com

truerelaxationwellnesscenter@yahoo.com

CHAPTER 10

The Twelve Steps on the Stairway to Heaven: The Path Out and Up from Food Addiction

Joni Berman

Food addiction is a topic that you may not have heard much about. A lot has been written about drug addiction, alcohol addiction, and even sex addition. However, food addiction is just as real and just as deadly physically, emotionally, mentally, and spiritually.

This is a discussion about the correlation between spiritual recovery from food addiction and the process of ascension. You may wonder what common thread could tie these two topics together. Simply stated, it is weight. In no way should this be considered a comprehensive explanation of either topic. For example, in order for a food addict to have a spiritual awakening, it is necessary for her to follow a set of instructions in concert with abstaining from all addictive eating, which includes limiting the amount she consumes. To do this she must follow a disciplined approach to eating. This article intentionally leaves out a discussion of food plans.

For the purposes of this article, most definitions of ascension will apply. I use the term food addict to refer to someone who is dependent upon processed foods, such as sugar, wheat, and flour. For ease of writing, I refer to a food addict as a "she," which in no way implies that there are no male food addicts.

A food addict suffers from a physical allergy coupled with a mental obsession. In other words, when a food addict eats addictively, she craves more. Once she begins to eat addictively the physical allergy is triggered and she has lost control over the amount she eats.

One may be curious as to why someone eats addictively if this process is guaranteed to be triggered every time she consumes the first bite. After all, a person suffering from a peanut allergy simply does not eat peanuts. The problem for the food addict is in her mind. The food addict's mind convinces her that *this* time a "bite" won't hurt. *This* time it will be different. *This* time the allergy won't be triggered. These thoughts are the mental obsession that guarantees a food addict will always pick up the first bite, thus making it impossible to simply abstain from certain foods, unless she can find help.

Before crossing the line into full-blown addiction, food had provided a sense of ease and comfort for her; food had served as the solution to all of life's problems. As her need for food progressed, it took more and more food to provide this ease and comfort. Eventually the food stops working and the addict is merely chasing an insatiable craving; there will never be enough food to sate the craving.

Once this stage of addiction is reached, the food addict is doomed. As soon as she starts eating, she has no power to stop. When stopped, she is guaranteed to start eating again. The mental obsession, which tells her to take the "bite," will eventually drive her back to the food. Now, food, which once served to provide ease and comfort for our food addict, is the source of much pain and anguish. A vicious cycle has developed, leaving a life destined to serving the master: food.

In *Alcoholics Anonymous* (hereafter referred to as the Big Book[1]), we are told that there is a solution to this "seemingly hopeless state of mind and body." It is not a physical solution – one cannot merely decide to stop eating so as not to trigger the craving. Nor is it behavioral – a person is unable to make a decision in the same mind which is ruled by obsession. Only a spiritual awakening can relieve this malady.

The Big Book describes a very specific spiritual awakening that is achieved as a result of taking the Twelve Steps, a process that opens the spiritual path to "lighten" the food addict and prepare her for ascension. I will briefly explain these directions, which are guaranteed to wake the sleeping spirit of a food addict.

A person whose life is controlled by food addiction is weighted down; stuck in her unchanging world; unmanageable. The heaviness of a life controlled by food is far greater than the excess pounds her body carries. Another way to see this is that she is living in a state of low vibration; afraid of change and afraid to evolve to a higher vibration. She is blocked from the sunlight of the spirit; afraid to ascend.

Many active food addicts experience chaotic lives - much like an alcoholic. Everyone knows or has heard stories of life with an alcoholic. Alcoholics are unable to maintain healthy relationships; have difficulty performing well in their jobs; are emotionally unpredictable; spend much of their time depressed; and are riddled with fear. All of this is true about active food addicts as well. Unable to control food, many food addicts have just about given up on ever living a better life.

When the pain of being stuck in this state becomes unbearable, a food addict may become ready to admit she is powerless to control this addiction. This admission has a tendency to leave an addict feeling extremely desperate and willing to do whatever it takes to find freedom from the control of food. The addictive life has not worked. Food no longer serves as a solution to life. All that happens to the food addict seeking relief in a bowl of ice cream is the need for more ice cream. She is unable *not* to eat addictively and eating only demands more and more eating. The food addict is hopeless. There seems to be no physical solution to escaping this cycle of doom. When our food addict makes this admission she has taken Step One:

We admitted we were powerless over food--that our lives had become unmanageable.

When a recovered food addict shares her experience with someone new on this path, it inspires hope that it may be possible to rise out of this cycle of doom. For the first time, the food addict is able to experience the promise that life can change; that there is some power, some force beyond her, that can change her current condition. This revelation corresponds to an elevation to a higher vibration and broadened consciousness. The light of optimism, this hope of restoration to sanity, is the second step on this path to freedom:

Came to believe that a Power greater than ourselves could restore us to sanity.

Having completed the second step, the food addict knows there is another way to live. For the first time, she has a choice to make about her path in life. She can continue to struggle to beat the unbeatable foe, eating her way to her death, or she can choose the spiritual path. This would seem to be a very simple choice; however, it means giving up the known for the unknown. It means believing that God can and will lead us to freedom if we seek Him.

Despite the horror of a life controlled by trips to the grocery store and fast-food joints, this decision will take serious deliberation. This is not simply a choice to switch to a new life. Rather, it is a serious commitment. Choosing the spiritual solution to food addiction, our addict will have to quit the life she knows and begin following a very specific set of directions. The third step in this rise from the bondage of food is a pledge to take all of the actions which are prescribed.

When the food addict makes this commitment to lighten her load, and move beyond the limited life of addiction, she has elected to give up the bondage of self-will. She has decided to give up control of her life in favor of being guided by a power greater than herself. The Big Book suggests the following prayer upon making this decision: "God, I offer myself to Thee-to build with me and to do with me as Thou wilt. Relieve me of the bondage of self, that I may better do Thy will. Take away my difficulties, that victory over them may bear witness to those I would help of Thy Power, Thy Love, and Thy Way of life. May I do Thy will always!"[2]

Having taken Step Three, our food addict has taken one more stride in her evolution and ascension out of food addiction:

Made a decision to turn our will and our lives over to the care of God as we understood Him.

Steps Four through Nine are considered the action steps in this journey out of food addiction. There are very specific actions that a food addict is directed to take in order to enter the world of the spirit. Completing the prescription is guaranteed to free the food addict from the bondage of food.

Having taken the third step, the food addict begins facing those things which are blocking her spiritual path and keeping her stuck in the dark world of low vibrations. Fear of what may be and resentment of what has been make it impossible for our food addict to show up, present, for her life.

The fourth step instructs the food addict to take a rigorous inventory of her resentments by completing a matrix. In the first column, she identifies each of the people, principles, and institutions, with whom she holds grudges, by name. After listing all of her resentments and fears, she is instructed to write the causes of the anger in the second column beside each name. She is then led through a process to discover why she resents and fears them.

In the third column, our food addict is instructed to write how she believes she has been hurt by each name on her list. Is her experience that her self-esteem, security, ambitions, personal or sex relations have been interfered with?

Then in the fourth column, the food addict is asked to look at each situation for the part she has played, putting out of her mind the wrongs others have done. In this revealing exercise, she looks for her own mistakes; where she has been selfish, dishonest, self-seeking, frightened, or inconsiderate. She then repeats this process listing all of her fears, and discovering where her faults allowed the fear to surface and block her from God's will.

Although this may sound like a very objective fact-finding assignment, many food addicts have great difficulty completing it. Even though it is a task which can be completed in a couple of hours, I have seen people drag it out for years. They are too fearful to see the truth about their life. Many food addicts balk at this step and return to the servitude of food. However, those who are truly willing to do whatever it takes to recover, persist in the effort. Once this process is completed, she has taken Step Four:

Made a searching and fearless moral inventory of ourselves.

After completing her inventory, it is critical that she review her work to ensure its completeness. All of the resentments, which have been blocking her from God, have limited her consciousness. Her energy has been focused on numbing the pain of her life rather than on making a connection with all that is. This unresolved anger and fear, which is extremely painful, has kept her eating addictively to manage her feelings. Her life has been heavy and dark.

In order to continue on this path, she is directed to acknowledge to God and another human being, all of this "stuff" which has been consuming her consciousness. Through this admission, she is able to see her shortcomings which create this ongoing pain in her life and slow her spiritual progress. In addition, she is able to see the harm she has caused to those around her.

Often, what was difficult to put on paper is even more difficult to acknowledge to another person. Those who do, see freedom and light. After having made this admission, she has taken Step Five:

Admitted to God, to ourselves and to another human being the exact nature of our wrongs.

The next instruction on the spiritual journey is to become ready to release all of the shortcomings which have been keeping her from being all that she could be; the traits which she has admitted are objectionable. According to the Big Book, addicts are selfish, self-centered people whose behavior is ego-driven. These characteristics block food addicts from the sunlight of the spirit.

Many of those on this path hesitate at this step. They are concerned that they will no longer recognize themselves if they give up these character defects. Step Six reads:

We're entirely ready to have God remove all these defects of character.

Soon after having completed this step, the process continues by asking to have all of these character defects removed. The Big Book suggests that our food addict make this request to God in a prayer such as: "My Creator, I am now willing that you should have all of me, good and bad. I pray that you now remove from me every single defect of character which stands in the way of my usefulness to you and my fellows. Grant me strength, as I go out from here, to do your bidding. Amen."[3] Having made this request, Step Seven has been accomplished:

Humbly asked Him (GOD) to remove our shortcomings.

Following asking for divine help, the food addict has more work to clean up the wreckage of her life. It is not merely enough to acknowledge the wrongs she has done; she must make them right. If she is to clear the pathway to the Source and be free of the negativity and darkness she has spread along her life's trail, she must make amends.

In reviewing her inventory, she makes a list of all of the people she has harmed – ignoring any harm that was done to her. This is about her and freeing herself, NOT about anyone else. She then lists the harms that she caused and notes whether or not she is willing to make them right.

Since making the decision in Step Three and committing to follow every direction, the steps are not optional, if she is to be free of the food addiction and follow a spiritual path.

Once she is willing, she has completed Step Eight:

Made a list of all persons we had harmed, and became willing to make amends to them all.

The next step requires making amends to all of those who have been harmed. This step is necessary for her to move beyond the pain of her past. As someone who has spent much of her past functioning at a low vibration, she most likely has spent much time apologizing for what she perceived to be her wrongs to others. This amend is different; change must happen with this amend.

To make amends, the food addict will make an appointment to speak with each of the people she has harmed. Here, the Big Book directs the food addict to express a "sincere desire to right the wrong."[4] Regardless of the circumstances, the food addict is willing to face each of the people and to discuss how she has harmed them AND do what she must to right the wrong.

Many food addicts have profound encounters with this step - marriages which seemed to have suffered irreparable differences, healed with one conversation; dread of consequences for deeds that had been done, vanished when responsibility was accepted. Friendships which had appeared to have been lost forever were mended and wrongs forgiven. Finishing amends, and being right with the world, is an amazing and freeing experience.

Having completed all of her amends, the food addict has taken Step Nine:

Made direct amends to such people wherever possible, except when to do so would injure them or others.

Once our food addict completes the action Steps, she has recovered from food addiction and has entered the world of the Spirit. She has ascended out of her resentments and fears and is no longer weighted down by her addictive eating. She is vibrating at a higher level and evolving spiritually. This is just the beginning of her spiritual path. The possibilities for growth and broadening of consciousness are endless.

The three remaining steps to be taken are a prescription for living a spiritual life. Through these daily practices anything is possible in the spiritual realm; there are no limits to how far our food addict can ascend.

In order to keep on this path, the direction is to continue to practice Steps Four thru Nine. These six steps are condensed into one step and practiced on a daily basis.

As one moves through life, she is to persist in taking inventory, looking only at her part. Whenever her ego takes over - when indulging in selfishness, dishonesty, resentment, or fear – she is to ask God at once to remove the problem behavior. She then needs to turn her thoughts to someone she can help. Living according to God's plan, there is no room for indulging in self – her life is now about doing God's work. "Love and tolerance of others is our code."[5] This process keeps her clear of the burden of resentments and is the daily practice of Step Ten:

Continued to take personal inventory and when we were wrong promptly admitted it.

The next instruction calls for daily prayer and meditation. This is our food addict's opportunity to expand her consciousness, to grow in her awareness of God, and to maintain fit spiritual condition. Each individual has limitless opportunity as she practices this step.

On one hand, a recovered food addict may simply choose to live above the limits of her ego-bound self, fully grounded in a practical reality guided by a power greater than she. On the other hand, someone may use these steps to ascend to a level of consciousness that knows Oneness with all that is. Practicing these principles opens the recovered food addict to endless possibility.

The practice of prayer and meditation is Step Eleven:

Sought through prayer and meditation to improve our conscious contact with God, as we understood Him, praying only for knowledge of His will for us and the power to carry that out.

The final charge to the recovered food addict is to continue to practice all of the previous steps. She is to help other suffering food addicts out of the morass of the dis-ease. She is to let them know there is hope and that they do not have to die a slave to cookies; that there is a way to ascend from the addiction to food.

Finally, she must continue to practice living life according to the principles outlined in the Big Book. Her life is no longer run on self-will; she is now to live according to God's will. As she does this she is practicing Step Twelve:

Having had a spiritual awakening as the result of these steps, we tried to carry this message to food addicts, and to practice these principles in all our affairs.

In summary, there is hope for an active food addict, **weighted** down by resentments, fears, and often excess pounds. When her load becomes so heavy that she is desperate to move out of that existence, she can rise up from her predicament. Only a spiritual experience, or spiritual awakening, as a result of rigorously following the prescribed course of action, will lead her to the light. As our food addict or any addict ascends the steps, following the simple but not easy set of instructions, she rises out of the darkness of addiction.

You may wonder how I can present this information with such conviction. You see, I know it is true. In 1990, I began my own personal journey out of food addiction. In 1991 my spiritual studies expanded beyond the Big Book. With many bumps along my path, I practice these steps every day. Following a healthy way of eating is preparing my physical body for ascension. Practicing these principles prepares me spiritually. This is a lifelong discipline, just as ascension is a life-long discipline.

Without the excess baggage or weight of an unmanageable life, all food addicts, including myself, are able to ascend to a level limited only by the infinite.

About Joni Berman

Joni Berman is a Reiki Master and ARCH Master. She began working with the Twelve Steps of Alcoholics Anonymous in 1990. She can be found living happily now and ever after, at home in Maryland. She may be contacted at joniberman@verizon.net.

Be the Energy

Trust the energy that courses
through you. Trust-then take
surrender even deeper.
Be the energy.

Don't push anything away.
Follow each sensation back to
its source and focus your awareness
there. Be the ecstasy.

Be unafraid of consummate wonder.
Emerge so new, so vulnerable,
that you don't know
who you are.

Be the energy, and paradoxically,
be at peace. Dare to be your own
illumination, and blaze a trail across
the clear night sky like lightning.

   Danna Faulds, *Prayers to the Infinite*

About Danna Faulds

Danna Faulds, poet and dedicated practitioner of Kripalu Yoga, is the author of four popular books of yoga poetry: *Go In and In; One Soul; Prayers to the Infinite;* and *From Root to Bloom.* A former librarian, Danna works part-time as an archivist at the Woodrow Wilson Presidential Library, does free-lance editing for Kripalu Center, and occasionally teaches writing workshops. She lives with her husband Richard in the Shenandoah Valley of Virginia, where they try to keep one step ahead of the weeds in their organic vegetable garden. She is currently working on a memoir titled *Into the Heart of Yoga* about her experiences with yoga and writing.

Danna writes about her practice: "The potent combination of meditation, yoga, and writing has brought lasting transformation into my life. I can't point to any one practice and say it's responsible, but together they have shifted just about everything about me.

The transformative process isn't always blissful. In fact, it is often profoundly uncomfortable, but when it really comes down to it, what else is there? Yoga and meditation fuel the fire, and writing gives me a way to read the smoke signals that rise up from inner experience. I take delight in reporting on the journey."

Danna's poetry books can be purchased on Amazon.com or directly from the author by emailing yogapoems@aol.com

CHAPTER 11

Ascension: Life at the Peaks

Alison Carter

WHAT IS ASCENSION?

An old man, with staff in hand, climbs a mountain. Step by step, he ascends, offering us an image of the simplest, dictionary definition of ascension: Going, moving, rising, climbing, evolving or growing upward. As humans, we are multi-dimensional beings with physical, emotional, mental, and spiritual levels. Each of our levels has its own inner staircase(s) or mountain(s) that we can climb, or ascend. It is exciting that we can develop awareness and skills to actively participate in our own ascension process. What I share, I've learned from listening within and from many teachers in this and other dimensions. This is my truth as I know it now. Take what speaks to you; just let the rest go.

The Peaks

We just love our peaks! We've all had them. We think of them as magic, blessed, and miraculous. They are not rushes induced by drugs or addictions. They are those moments when we are high on life; at the top of our game. We can do no wrong. We love everyone; everyone loves us. We speak from our heart in a stream of consciousness and profoundly touch others. We are in the zone, flowing, moving, grooving, producing, creating and expressing. We are spirited, full of joy, connected and passionate; visionaries following our dream. We are truth; we understand; we accept; we just know. We're home within the cosmos and can't imagine not living in this space forever.

Then............................we crash!

Darn.

After climbing, sweating and somehow getting "there," what a bummer that with the next breath, we slide back down a slippery slope, right back into our old boxes of fear, criticism, unhappiness, or whatever other density we had briefly overcome. How do we get to the peak and stay there?

As a flower child of the '60s, I first read about "peak experiences" and self actualization from psychologist and philosopher Abraham Maslow. My inner voice, my Spirit, whispered a great question to me:

"Were these brief, lofty states, these moments of grace, actually gifts from Spirit -- *teasers*, given to us to whet our appetites and show us greater possibilities in life?"

That whisper launched a major life quest for me. It intrigued me to imagine if it was possible that we could:

♥ Grow beyond these magic moments just "happening" to us;

♥ Grow beyond being the passive passenger on the magic carpet ride, being transported to these incredible life moments by forces outside ourselves; and

♥ Grow into the Magician, who weaves the magic and rides the peaks on our own.

I mused further. If we could create peaks, we could build more magic moments into our lives. Then . . . if we got really good at it, maybe we could have longer retreats or eventually live up on the mountain tops. . .

Now I know we can participate in creating these experiences; they need not be totally random or hopelessly beyond our control. In this chapter, we'll explore some ways we can facilitate our ascension process by using tools that make us lighter so we can rise to the peaks brightening our vibrations by loving ourselves with Radical Self Care©, attuning to vibes so we can use our built-in guidance system to make choices, and getting quiet so we can hear the soft subtle input from our Spirits that support us to live our best life.

Ascension is not new to us. It is part of evolution, of our inner drive to grow, know, to be fulfilled. Many of us have worked very hard on ourselves to advance in the adventures of life. We've experimented with regimens for physical care. We've explored movement, massage, acupuncture, cleaning our systems, and energy healing. We've gone to therapy, studied self-help, learned empowerment tools, attended workshops, read books, cleared old emotions, forgiven, healed relationships, practiced gratefulness, expressed truth, created in multi-media, and rewritten our life scripts. The list goes on.

These personal growth resources taught us conscious ways to grow and care for our bodies, minds, emotions and spirits. We gained an arsenal of tools that help us create conditions within us that facilitate entering higher states, giving us more tastes of the delightful flavors of our possibilities. While these expansions into new human territory are significant in helping to mark paths to the peaks, most of our peak visits are still temporary and quite short-lived. Living our best life can be hard to attain and impossible to sustain, especially if we ignore, neglect, or mistreat any level of our selves.

Our physical, emotional, mental and spiritual levels are the foundation for human life. These levels are distinct, yet interrelated. What we do or don't do on one level, affects all the other levels.

For example, if I:

- neglect my body - my emotions dull, mind wanders; I have no energy to channel the fire of my Spirit.
- take excellent care of my body - I think better; handle emotions, express my Spirit.
- bury feelings - I distort thinking, manifest illness, dim Spirit.
- ignore my Spirit - I make choices that bring unhappiness, trauma, or illness.
- focus only on Spirit - I create imbalance.

Soon, I'll be sliding back down the mountain again.

I am convinced that our ability to create and sustain higher ascended states for longer stretches depends on creating a solid life foundation with practices that include the principles in "Radical Self Care©."

Radical Self Care©

Radical Self Care© is "radical" because it is a paradigm shift in how we think about caring for ourselves. With Radical Self Care©, we develop individualized systems of self-care, where we monitor our physical, emotional, mental and spiritual levels with regular, scheduled check-ins, and self-care maintenance throughout every day.

We are conscious that multi-leveled self-care builds the strong life foundation that is the essential base for ascension and living our best life. Therefore, we assign committed top priority to our well-being, and take the necessary actions to monitor and care for ourselves on every level throughout every day.

Many of us were taught to put ourselves last; to take care of others' needs before our own. We must adopt the policy that in the airplane of life, we put the oxygen mask on ourselves first, and then we will have the energy to help others. Trying to ascend without adequate self care is like a tree reaching for the sky without adequate roots; we're just not ready or strong enough to hold the higher vibrations. With Radical Self Care© we fortify and ground our foundation as the solid base from which we can ascend; we build strength that enables us to sustain higher vibrations for longer periods.

In my journey, I've heard many wise spiritual teachers say: "Love your self." But how do I love me, when I don't love me? My frustration built as I never got much useful help about **how** to love myself.

At our wedding, my husband and I shared a story from Stephen Covey's book, *Seven Habits of Highly Successful People*. Stephen wrote about a man who asked him for advice about what to do, as he had fallen out of love with his wife. Stephen said, "Love her." The man says again, "I repeat, I don't love her. How do you love, when you don't love?" Stephen said again, "Love her. Love is a verb. Love - the feeling – is the fruit of love. . ."

Here was a powerful clue for HOW to love our selves. When we love our selves as the verb love, we take the actions of caring for ourselves, which then produces the fruit, the feeling of loving ourselves.

With Radical Self Care©, we attend to all levels of ourselves with priority and consistency. These actions of self care will bring us the fruit of love, the feeling of loving ourselves. When we love ourselves, we live in higher vibrations based on a solid foundation that is necessary for life at the peaks. Self love is not egotism or disregard for others. We love others only after we truly love ourselves.

Daily Routine Maintenance of All Levels

We know our body requires constant maintenance throughout each day. But we may not be fully aware that our emotions, mind and spirit also require routine maintenance throughout the day or they also malfunction.

I recommend examining our self care practices, as they can be rote, superstitious, or inconsistently applied rather than integrated throughout every day. Remember, if any level needs care, the performance of all levels is affected detrimentally. The challenge is to integrate what we already know about taking care of ourselves into daily routine maintenance for all our levels.

Great News: Easily Incorporate Radical Self Care© Into Daily Life!

There were years when I grabbed fast food and worked through meals to meet grant application deadlines. I juggled home, child, pets, relationships, job, evening teaching and healing work. I actually had a book of "To Do" Lists.

If I had heard my own message back then, I would have shrieked, "Radical Self Care© – you've got to be kidding. My lists are birthing baby lists. I cannot do one more thing!" If you're feeling the burden, there's great news. Radical Self Care© can easily be incorporated into daily life. Here's the secret.

Though we may not be perfect in how we care for our bodies, basic physical care can't be ignored. We have to breath, eat, sleep, rest, go to the bathroom, etc. Of necessity, we're trained as kids in physical caretaking, so these habits are more ingrained than taking care of ourselves on the other levels. The key to incorporation of Radical Self Care© is to link the care of our emotional, mental and spiritual levels, to necessary, routine body care.

Examples of Linkages:

-- Washing hands or showering: Imagine every level cleaned as dirty vibes wash down the drain.

-- Grooming: Notice what's right about you, compliment you, build self-esteem.

-- In the bathroom: Grab the quiet moment alone, close your eyes, and listen to your heart.

-- Eating: Check your levels; give your spirit soul food.

-- Greeting others: Declare, thereby claiming: "I am having a fantastic day."

-- Walking: Listen to what you say to you. Be positive and nurturing.

-- Doing chores: Play music, sing, and involve your inner child to engage Spirit.

-- Paying bills: Practice gratitude - the great transformer of negatives.

-- Shopping: Decide things you'll do to be of service to others.

-- Planning: Rehearse future successes - see, feel, sense great outcomes now.

-- Anytime: Live, relive and celebrate successes, fun and joys in full color - no matter how small.

You get the idea. Make up your own linkages that easily integrate Radical Self Care© for you. **Very important**: Have fun with it! Make it a game. Engage your inner child.

Consider making a commitment to your own version of Radical Self Care©. Be aware and take actions, every day, throughout the day, to routinely maintain your physical, emotional, mental and spiritual levels. Pay attention to important clues like: stress, fatigue, anxiety, nervousness, unhappiness, confusion, grouchiness, feeling out of sorts, ungrounded, lost; dropping energy levels, etc.

When you check-in with your self, ask questions such as: What's happening with me now - physically, emotionally, mentally, and spiritually? What do I need on each level? Then take the actions required.

Radical Self Care© supports ascension as it is self love in action and helps us create a healthy rounded foundation for life. As we attune to all our levels, it is also helps us to be in touch with wholeness and oneness within ourselves. This awareness can expand to our connection with others, so we fully experience the oneness of all. Increasing awareness, connection and oneness, raises our consciousness, lifts our vibration and we ascend upward.

Radical Self Care© is a necessary ingredient for ascension. Without this mastery of self, there is no sustaining life at the peaks as we'll easily stumble on the pebbles, lose balance, and roll back down the hill. Radical Self Care© is mastery of our foundation from which we express, create and fulfill our Being.

Getting to Know Energy Vibrations

Everything in the universe is energy. As energy beings, humans have an energy field in and around the body called an aura. Our aura reflects every aspect of us - our consciousness, thoughts, intellect, physical condition, intention, clarity, confusion, emotions – everything, from every level; it's all there in our energy.

We are all wired to feel and sense energies to varying degrees. Most children and some adults can also see, hear, smell or taste energies. We refer to our ability to sense energy as intuition, gut feeling, vibes, sixth sense, or inner voice. Awareness of energy basics can empower the magician within to bring more magic into our lives.

Good Vibes

Our energy reflects our consciousness. When we're focused on the uplifting aspects of life, we feel better and others sense and are attracted to our "good vibes." The vibration of higher consciousness is refined, delicate, yet strong, and literally vibrates at a higher rate. Higher energies are clear, smooth, balanced, expansive, shiny, symmetrical, and full of pretty colors and beautiful bright light. Many spiritual traditions talk about being **enlightened**. When our energies are "in light," we are en-light-ened; living predominantly in ascended consciousness.

Consciousness ascends as we increase: love, compassion, respect, peace, understanding, wisdom, truth, creativity, play, caring, serving, giving, gratitude, forgiveness, empowering support, fulfillment, laughter, mining treasures in life's pains, health, expanded vision, expression of Spirit's passion, etc.

Bad Vibes

In contrast, when we're focused on the darker side of life, we descend, go backwards, and hang out in darkness and density, with: war, violence, abuse, addictions, greed, slander, revenge, hatred, murder, rape, manipulation, betrayal, judgment, lying, hurtful intent, sickness, struggle, poverty, fear, etc.

These lower energies feel dense, blocked, dark, heavy, jagged, imbalanced, broken, thick, asymmetrical, and filled with static and debris. The colors are cloudy, muddy, dark, and unpleasant. We experience these energies as "bad vibes."

"Bad" is not used here to judge anyone's worth or inherent value, but as a descriptor of energies we sense that are not in our own best interest.

We're all a mixture of good and bad vibes. No one escapes bad vibes. We're irritable; the kids are yelling; we're late; the other driver cuts us off. We ascend to our best life as we incorporate more ascending aspects of consciousness and decrease the descending *aspects.*

Natural Law of Attraction

When we get on a dark track, things can escalate downhill. This is because under natural law, like attracts like. The unhappy energies we're giving out attract more unhappiness back to us. We're unkind to the checkout clerk, so she hisses back at us. Give grief, get grief. Remembering this multiplier factor in the Law of Attraction can be a great motivator to work our way back to more positive states.

The same law also applies to the good in our life. Light, bright consciousness attracts more of the same and lifts us up to the high life. Give smiles, get smiles.

Using Our Internal Guidance System

Science now confirms that everything is energy. We all can sense energy. We know the difference between good vibes that make us feel good and elevate us, and bad vibes that make us feel bad and bring us down. This awareness is built into us and is part of our internal guidance system. But how do we develop this awareness and use it in practical ways in daily life? Unfortunately, many of us have lost the operations manual for this vital inner human sonar.

In ancient history, survival dictated that tribal leaders be chosen for their sensitive internal guidance systems. They could use their vibes to alert their people to predators, find food, discover healing plants, discern poison, pick the best place to live and warn when to skedaddle to avoid disaster.

Fortunately, we still embody this internal guidance system in our awareness of energy, which enables us to sense "good" and "bad" vibes through gut reactions and intuitions. Our built-in survival system is a rich heritage and one of the most powerful tools we have to enhance our lives.

Our lives are filled with choices. If we become masterful in using our internal guidance system, we are empowered from within to check vibes and assess the energy of our options. Our innate powers can help guide the hundreds of choices we make every day that impact our well-being; the so called day to day "small" choices (like what we choose to eat), that accumulate into life styles and habits with significant consequences, and those "bigger" choices (like career) that set major life courses.

Like our ancestors, we can plug into our built-in vibe guidance system and increase our awareness of the energy of everything around us to help keep us safe, and guide us to make better choices. As we make more good choices and take better care of ourselves, we raise our vibrations.

Following are some tools I find useful to activate and/or build skill in using our vibe guidance system. When practicing, start with choices of little consequence until you sharpen skills and build confidence; then work up to bigger life decisions. As you practice, be adamant; there are no failures. Every experience is valuable. Adopt a playful spirit; be like a kid playing a fun game.

Vibe Sensing Warm Up

--Shake your hands like you are shaking off dirt.

--Put your palms together and rub briskly.

--Slowly separate hands noticing sensations between them.

--Repeat a number of times, bringing palms close together and apart - slowly, gently.

--Notice feelings and sensations between your hands: warmth, coolness, tension, static, like pulling and relaxing rubber bands, or other sensations.

What you feel between your palms is how your guidance system gives you information and feedback.

Extreme Practice – Terrific and Terrible

To activate and train awareness to sense good and bad vibes, choose extremes to help clarify how you personally get feedback.

1. Gather items that you know are:

   Terrific - healthy enlivening food, fabrics you love to touch, music or books that inspire

   Terrible - rotten food, insecticides, or toxins for you

2. Do the Vibe Sensing Warm Up.

3. Sense each "terrible" item first and then sense each "terrific" item.

   Sense items by holding each in your hand, one at a time. Then sense the energy in the ½ to 5 or more inch space around each item.

   Remember to clear energy from your hands by shaking and clapping them between each sensory experience with each item. Repeat the Vibe Sensing Warm Up if you get confused or lose touch with feeling the energy or sensing the difference between the items.

4. Note all your sensations with every item. How does the energy feel? Be aware of any feelings, sensations, reactions, images, smells, sounds, colors, static, etc. What do you sense, see, hear, taste, imagine?

   Note differences in how your body senses "terrific" and "terrible" items.

Once you understand the feedback your guidance system gives you to distinguish between good and bad vibes, practice with as many items as possible. You might check two types of foods energetically; then taste test to verify and refine your skills. Check the vibes of salt, vinegar, sugar, sweets, coffee. Look for variables like organic, brands, additives. Don't presume results. The more you practice, the more skilled you will become with noticing and interpreting subtleties.

Vibe sensing can direct us to what is good for us that may not conform to others' expectations. I've been criticized for drinking coffee, but I brushed off the raised eyebrows and snide remarks, sensing that moderate coffee in moderation was fine for me. Now, research affirms coffee is indeed very good for me since it slows a neurological disease that runs in my family. My body knew.

Bad Vibe Danger Alerts

Bad vibes warn us when something or someone is not good for us and range from mildly disturbing, to intense warnings of danger, when we need to run, not walk, away.

I'll never forget the day the pharmacist handed me my prescription, and it energetically burned my hand - not a good vibe! My body is extremely sensitive to medications and my doctor forgot that a certain drug had caused blood clots for me. Because the energy burned my hand, I looked up the medication and found it was a generic of the drug I can't take. Bless those vibes!

On another day, I was coming back to my office from lunch. I got on the elevator and suddenly felt a gripping cold chill and a queasy stomach. Instead of ignoring the feelings, I bolted back out the elevator door and ran toward the lobby guard station. I looked back to see two men, who had been in the elevator with me, running at high speed toward the building exit. Days later, there was a robbery and rape in that building. The victim's description of her attackers matched the men who were in the elevator with me. I still bless my vibes' danger warning that saved me from harm.

Such warnings are not unusual. Crime victims frequently say they felt something wrong; the hair stood up on their arms; they had cold chills, bad feelings, bad vibes and a strong impulse to run. Learning to value and respond to our internal guidance system can keep us out of situations that are unhealthy or unhappy paths for us.

Most bad vibes are not so intense; they are very subtle. They signal us with mild unpleasantness, a twinge of discomfort, or uneasiness. These cues may be barely noticeable unless we practice quieting skills so that we can hear them, and wise-up to notice vibe alerts. Until we recognize them as the vital markers on the path of our lives that they truly are, we may ignore the gentle inner promptings that we need a course correction.

Vibe mastery practiced in small ways can lead to mastery in the larger decisions and arenas of life. We graduate from picking the tastiest apple to picking friends, mates, homes, cars, travel routes, colors, restaurants, jobs, animal companions - the applications are endless. Once you understand how you sense good and bad vibes, you can use the information to take better care of yourself and consistently make choices that raise your vibration. Practicing can be great fun. Enjoy!

SSSSHHHH; LISTENING REQUIRES QUIET

Many spiritual teachers instruct: "Listen to your heart," but that phrase sounded pat and hit me the same way as being told to "love myself." I was clueless how to listen to my heart and could never get much useful instruction that worked for me. But this message is vital to living our best life, as it directs us to our heart space where our Spirit lives. Listening to the advice of our Spirit is another essential ingredient for ascension. But first we must be able to hear what our Spirit is saying to us, which is nearly impossible over the din of busy minds and endlessly chatty egos. To hear, we must learn to quiet the mind and ego.

Meditation is often the first quieting tool suggested. It's hard to find a better one, but I resisted - mightily. For years, I made myself sit in my meditation corner, often peeking at the clock, waiting out my sentence. Near the meditations ending, I usually quieted. But the unhappiness I felt getting there did not jive with my truth that Spirit is joyful.

I needed to change my meditation paradigm from one of grinding duty and discipline, to one where I looked forward to and cherished quiet time. Since motivation comes from what we get that is useful, fun, joyful or rewarding, I looked at what we can get from meditation that is so juicy, we wouldn't miss it for anything. The motivators are priceless. How about:

--Lovely quiet, a time treasure just for me; a moment of peace to restore balance.

--A chance to listen to my heart; to ask questions and get answers from Spirit; dialogue with my wise self; tap the secrets of the universe.

--A chance to reset our systems back to truth as the stillness in meditation functions like rebooting the computer after error codes come up.

--Or, as Sonia Choquette, teacher, psychic, author, suggested at a conference - Meditation is our "chance to climb up on God's lap and hang out."

Not bad return on a few minutes investment of time!

Now that we're clearly motivated, how do we shut up and be quiet? There are many meditation approaches, CDs, and music that can help us to quiet and are fun to explore. Find what works for you and do it every day, as needed, in moments throughout the day. Start with a few minutes; work up to 10-20 minutes, if you can.

Note: If sitting still is not your bag, consider other style meditations – be in nature, walk, dance, sing, create, or engage in mindful activities. Some are empowered meditating in groups.

Here are my simple, fast- acting favorites that came to me in my quiet time and they work like charms. Try them.

Quieting: SSSSHHHH

--Whisper sssssshhhhhhhhhhhhhh to yourself.

--Hear the voices in your head quieting.

--Get ready to hear from the most important being in your life – your Spirit.

--Actively listen with quiet anticipation.

Remember what sssshhhh does when someone sssshhhh's a noisy audience. Within moments, there is quiet and the audience goes into an active listening stance. After quieting by sssshhhh-ing myself for a couple of months, I went to a workshop taught by a Tibetan Llama who said that sssshhhh is the universal sound that shuts down noise! My inner voice that suggested this awesomely powerful tool for quieting was right on target.

Holding the Vessel

1. Clear intent backed with physical action is powerfully hard to beat in manifesting our goals in life.
2. Intend to quiet.
3. Then act by putting your hands on both sides of your head over your ears.
4. Sense all the movement inside, picturing or feeling it as disturbed water in a container, a storm on a lake, turbulence in a pond.
5. See or feel it quickly settling down to stillness.
6. Be in still quiet.
7. When thoughts reactivate, see the water ripples quickly running their course to be still again.
8. Imagine your hands holding quiet.
9. Feel the turbulence settle from the calm in your hands.
10. Be quiet. It's the only way you can hear your Spirit's guidance.

Clearing Your Heart♥

If you have trouble getting clear messages from your inner voice, it may mean that your heart area has dense unhappy energies blocking your flow. Try this quick clearing to re-open the channel between your highest spiritual aspects and your body.

--Say out loud your intention to clear your communication channel to hear Spirit.

--Invite your Spirit to be fully at home in your heart and fully present in your body.

--Take several deep breaths.

While inhaling deeply, imagine that you are pulling in the beautiful bright light of your Spirit through the top of your head, down to your heart.

As you exhale, make a long audible haaaaaaaaaaaa sound and imagine that the air clears any darkness or blocks in the center of your chest, clearing your heart.

--Give thanks for the presence of your Spirit and have your conversation with Spirit.

Summary: Ascension in this Life

We are Spirits, temporarily housed in the temples of our Earthly physical bodies.

Ascension is Spirit fully present within our hearts and awake in our body; it is **not** Spirit out of body.

Ascension is a process, not a completed task. We are never fully ascended, as we can always further refine our vibes.

Ascension within our humanity allows us to fully expand awareness, love and oneness with "all our relations" – a Native American reference to our rock, plant, animal, human, angelic and cosmic families; and we can participate in Mother Earth's ascension.

Ascension occurs as we refine and raise vibrations inside our temples. We facilitate our ascension by loving ourselves with Radical Self Care ©, attuning to vibrations to use our built-in guidance system for making choices, and quieting to hear Spirit in our hearts.

We are all Masters bringing higher energies into physical life. Eventually, we will reach and sustain enlightened states where we become the star that we are.

- ✪ Our possibilities are infinite; we are only limited by how much good we can stand.
- ✪ Ascension is heaven on Earth; it is time to create it now.
- ✪ Let it begin in me.
- ✪ How much heaven can we stand right now?

About Alison Carter

Alison Carter is author, playwright, healer, gatekeeper, and teacher, working with individual and planetary transformation and ascension. She lives in Berkeley Springs, West Virginia, with husband Sandy, and six Master Cats. Workshops include: Walking Stargates, Tending Our Spirits, Vibe Checks, Energy 101, Advanced Energy Healing, CoCreation and Ascension Now. She can be reached at 304-258-8430.

CHAPTER 12

The Path of Ascension

Dawn Fleming

The path of ascension may sound too far out there for some people to even consider; however, everyone on the planet is walking this path. Some just appear to move faster than others. The universe supports our ascension on all levels. The Ascended Masters provide love, encouragement and assistance for those willing to ask, listen and receive. An unlimited amount of energy, which is constantly increaseing in frequency, is being sent to us all the time by the universe to assist humanity's evolution. As a result, the shift in consciousness that is needed for ascension is happening. The most minimal effort on our part will provide vast rewards in ascending the quagmire of dense energy that plagues our planet. There are many things that we can do to accelerate the ascension process. Just about everything that I am going to discuss in this chapter, anyone can do. So there really is hope for all of us.

The great part about this journey is that as we are lifted into higher realms of truth and wisdom, the impact is experienced on various levels by all life on the planet. Just our aligning to the higher frequencies of light and ascension helps humanity and the planet transition into the higher dimensions.

You can read this whole chapter in one setting, or you can read each part separately and work with it. If you choose to read the whole chapter at once, I recommend that you go back and spend time working with each of processes. Spend a few days or more on each section.

Aligning with the process

Choose to align your body, mind, and emotions with the ascension energy. Every morning, settle into the awareness that this higher energy, in which you live and breathe, is guiding you to create heaven on earth in all areas of your life; supporting your ascension, humanity's and the planet's ascension. Sit in the knowing that this is the energy of your I AM Presence, which you were birthed from and will reunite with in this lifetime, once more, for eternity. That is a lot to sit with! Just be with this for a while and eventually it will become a knowing within your whole being. You will then see the world through the lens of ascension or your I AM Presence, where you will raise every relationship, interaction, and challenge to a higher level for solutions that come from love, compassion, peace, integrity, and oneness.

Use your breath to bring into your body the ascension energy every morning. Allow this exercise to cleanse your cells and energy field of the residue of dense energies from the day before. When you get a sense that your energy field is cleared, begin breathing in the ascension energy and allow it to fill every cell. Feel the energy and support. As you would fill your car with gas to fuel it for the day, breathe in the ascension energy, bringing light and powerful energy to fuel your entire being. When you sense that your body has absorbed its maximum quotient of this energy, breathe the ascension energy into the energy field around your body.

Start by sending the energy down to the area surrounding your feet, filling the space all around you out to three feet. Continue to focus on filling the entire space all around you from your feet to about three feet over your head. When you are finished, feel yourself enveloped in the loving embrace of this energy that supports your journey of ascension. Each time that you go through this process, you expand the quotient level of light that you are able to maintain and facilitate in your entire being.

Aligned with the awareness that we are this energy, and using the breath to facilitate this process, leads us to the next step.

Conscious evolution of purpose

The path of ascension becomes a conscious approach that continuously evolves and opens us to higher levels of understanding and being. As we walk this ascension path, we become more introspective. We begin to go within and observe our behaviors, thought patterns, and reactions to our world. Taking responsibility for our actions is one of the results of going within. Seeing the destructive patterns that have become automatic in our life, we begin to consciously make different choices that support a life aligned with the ascension energy. The light that we are bringing in through the first process opens our consciousness to wanting to make better choices and helps to balance us and lift us out of the negative energies. We get in touch with our goals and align ourselves with the energy that will support them. Our actions then come from a place within that is centered in a deep knowing and peace, and we extend this light, truth, and love to those around us. As our awareness expands, our consciousness fully develops into ascension consciousness; we embody the capacity to think, feel, and extend only the higher qualities of thoughts, feelings, and energy, which have a positive lifting effect and influence on all situations.

The "negative" egoic aspects of our behavior then have less control over us. Living in a place of being guided from the Source of this energy, we are able to fulfill our purpose as Lightworkers and World Servers. We are consciously able to align all of our being to serve our purpose with clarity and single-mindedness that is guided by wisdom.

Living in this state of consciousness lifts us into knowing that we exist to fulfill a higher plan, and frees us to live accordingly; not entrapped by the standards and requirements of society. Our life path may look the same, i.e. career, hobbies, and relationships; however, we are guided by a higher state of consciousness. We are free to respond to what is necessary in this moment of time. Our consciousness attunes to the higher airwaves. We can hear when we are called and we answer. Even if we do not hear, there is a knowing within us that propels us forward to fulfill our role.

Impact of these changes

As I said earlier, things are speeding up. This means the physical, emotional, and mental changes that we are going through are moving just as quickly to assist us in making these leaps in consciousness. On the energetic level, you are being restructured and rewired. Okay, you say. This process can be overwhelming at times. It might last a few minutes to a few days, or the process could take months to complete. It just depends on how much restructuring and integration is needed.

Overwhelmed is a good word to describe how I felt as I went through an intensive seven-week rewiring. Since I have the gift of actually seeing the energy field at times, I was able to see my energy field being taken apart and restructured over several days. At first, I thought that I might be leaving the planet. Then I was able to witness the new geometry that was built in its place. During this period I was exhausted and anxious. I typically am a very high-energy person without using caffeine. I have been referred to as the Energizer Bunny, and have been known to go all day and all night feeling energized and focused. So laying around on the sofa was not a typical scenario for me. The first shift lasted seven days.

I had a week reprieve before the next shift began, which lasted five weeks. I witnessed specific areas of my body release old, blocked-up energy and become restructured and rewired. After each area went through this series of changes, there was an integration period that followed. This whole process was difficult, to say the least, for all levels of my being.

On the physical level, I had aches and pains and a lot of pressure in several areas of my body, particularly around the heart, throat, and third eye. I had various tightening and releasing sensations around whatever area was being worked on that day or night. As the old energies were leaving, the memories that went with them surfaced. It was as if I was processing the past in fast-forward. There was no time to go over each issue. I just had to let them go, beyond forgiveness, to the total release of the energy. This alone was exhausting and overwhelming at times. Tears of sadness and joy were released. What a roller coaster ride this was! As the integration portion of the process was occurring, I was impacted on the mental level. I was able to see and understand why my old way of thinking and behaving was not serving me. I was aligning with a new consciousness and comprehending the necessity for it. Although part of me wanted to fight this, the truth of me knew that I had to release that old unconscious way of being and align with this higher truth.

I spent the majority of seven weeks on the sofa or in bed, witnessing this process. It was not easy, and in hindsight, I know this to be one of the most important events that has impacted my spiritual path. This shift was followed by several other shorter shifts over the following months. They opened me to higher levels of knowing, deepened my connection to the ascended beings, and strengthened my resolve as a Lightworker. I was gifted with a higher or more expanded consciousness and the courage to respond to life in new ways that support ascension for all.

However these changes occur within you, prayer and meditation can assist your process. Also, receive some energy and bodywork to help you to ground and integrate the changes. Be good to yourself during this time period, and set clear boundaries so that you can create the space to complete the process. Do not judge yourself for what surfaces during this process, but be very loving and gentle. These words of wisdom have stayed with me, as they are very relevant to integrating and working with the ascension energy - an ongoing process.

These changes are happening to all of us. Some people will experience the changes faster and more intensely than others. Some of us are aware of the process occurring, while others are not. In my healing practice, I see the restructuring going on all the time with my clients. I can tell who the clients are that are consciously working with the ascension energy. At times, I have seen the patterns change overnight. Not everyone will experience the degree of physical and emotional stress that I encountered. My intention in sharing this information is to educate you on this unfolding process and how it might look, not to scare you.

Many people are choosing to resist the process. They are so accustomed to the dense energy that they will decide to leave the planet rather than to evolve with it. Being comfortable with the familiarity of the negativity in their lives, they fear the thought of change. Somehow, they believe giving this up would leave them lost and out of alignment with those in their lives. We cannot force anyone to change. However, some who resist these changes may sink to the brink of death, only to experience an epiphany. In this experience they are rebirthed, seeing life through new eyes and feeling comfortable with the new vibration. Others will not and will choose to leave rather than evolve and ascend.

The integration of the new patterns of higher frequency energy is impacting all realms of life on our planet. Everyone and every living thing is being repatterned and rewired to create a realm of peace and beauty on the planet. It is not as if we have to go somewhere else to experience ascension. It can happen right here in the physical vehicle that we now embody. A new matrix of light is embracing humanity and our planet. In welcoming the energy of ascension, we embrace the changes that it brings for our total transformation and healing.

Living in the landscape of light

Going through this cycle of evolution, we continue to look for ways to live in the light, and to mesh our daily routine with the joy, peace, and harmony that is a natural extension of this ascension energy. We do not want to just have moments of joy and harmony in our meditation, and stress and frustration in dealing with the world. We want to integrate this ascension energy with all of our experiences, whether they are mundane tasks or thrilling experiences. We want to be living in and responding from this ascension light more than fifty percent of our time in order to achieve the greatest effect in aligning us with the realms of our I AM presence. In this space we begin to create a landscape of light all around us, paving the way for others to make this shift much easier.

One approach to expressing this ascension energy is to identify the qualities that are associated with experiencing this energy. These qualities include joy, harmony, peace, love, compassion, honor, grace, illumination, clarity, truth, abundance, transcendence, and healing, to name a few. Begin your day by aligning with any of these qualities. Meditate and pray on them. Feel the landscape of light awakening in you each morning as an ascension flame of light encompassing your whole being. Set the intention to keep this ascension flame alive within you all day and night. See your inner altar centered in your heart with the core of this flame burning and glowing. It might even look violet with gold around the edges. These are the colors associated with the high frequency of ascension energy. The ascension flame is feeding you all day long, keeping you attuned to the higher order of living, and keeping you from descending into the dense energies that create fear and paralysis.

Working with meditation, prayer and intention sets our course for the day. It begins to get easier to display these higher vibrational qualities. Not that we never get pulled into negative situations. It is just that our evolved consciousness aligned in our I AM Presence chooses not to stay in that space very long. We know there is another way to handle it without having to create chaos. Our consciousness embraces the higher qualities and goes within for the right action to take to address the situation. Bringing in the ascension energy lifts the situation to a higher level for resolution.

Each time something like this happens, the time harboring negativity will get shorter and shorter. The ascension light that is fed by our daily inner activities will be so strong that it will come forward to shine light onto the negative condition. It will give you the strength and courage to handle any situation with compassion and honor for yourself and others.

Your inner landscape of the active ascension flame begins to redesign your outer world. Manifestation becomes easy and almost instantaneous. The issues that have plagued you for a lifetime vanish. You are able to handle even more difficult situations that present themselves. You become a healer for your family, community and the planet. This is not limited to hands on healing. There are many Lightworkers and World Servers doing healing work that does not involve laying on of hands. They are active in the world taking their light into their jobs and community in: the government, schools, the grocery stores, hair salons, etc. Think about the earth angels that you have met in the most unlikely places.

The changes within your inner landscape will have you speaking your truth and sharing wisdom. You begin to see how living from this higher perspective makes a difference. You know that there is no alternative to living in alignment with this ascension energy. Eventually you will no longer see any of the alternatives, as your inner and outer worlds reflect the same ascension light. Society will no longer have a hold over how you live, respond, and move about the outer world. One with the ascension light, you are free to live your Truth, which creates harmony and peace.

Feeding the ascension flame

Every time that you have the opportunity, bring your consciousness into a state of divine love. The energy of love is so powerful that it can move mountains; an energy that propels us to ascend. It takes us to new heights of understanding where we know love is the landscape of the new world order that the ascension energy is designing. Love is the foundation for all that is real.

Working with the energy of love feeds the ascension flame within us, and it also reflects and feeds the flame in others. This is a way to truly accelerate the planetary ascension process. It also lifts us to knowing our oneness with all the Ascended Masters working to assist earth's ascension process. Love connects us through all the dimensions of time and space. Love heals our past and paves the way for transmutation and transformation. The alchemical reaction of love energy generates healing, and builds the foundation of the new structure in which an ascended humanity will live.

Just one act of divine love can create tremendous healing. Take a moment to imagine the positive impact of your continuous love flowing into the planet.

St. Germain offers a perspective

St. Germain is a master alchemist who teaches how to create change. He offered me these words of wisdom:

"You are a bundle of energy moving, shooting, and firing through the body, blessing or destroying the perfection that was given at birth. This energy bundle is an expression of thoughts, feelings, and prayers. Where the mind goes, the energy follows. When the mind centers on prayer-filled expressions, your life unfolds in the flow of the Divine. Centering on love, peace and joy, you are lifted into higher expressions of the Divine. In the stillness of the simplicity of prayer for love, peace, and joy, you become the Light language of energy that weaves patterns of these higher qualities around you and in you. You are charged with an incredible power that changes your life permanently. In the moments of Union, knowing this love, peace, and joy that you prayed for, you feel and know the Presence of God in you in that instant. You know that all is unfolding in Divine Order. When you can keep your prayer-filled mind and body actively reflecting and connecting with these feelings throughout the day, God's Light and Love for you begins to charge you and change you. God moves you and it feels right -- as if there were no other way."

Union with the ascension light

The next step in this evolutionary process is conscious Union with the ascension energy. Instead of being in the act of seeking to be love, peace, harmony, etc., you become the sacredness of the energy of these qualities. You enter the inner chamber of stillness at the center of the ascension flame; the Union where there is no separation between you and the ascension energy. You become what it is that you seek, whether it is love, peace, compassion, etc. You embody the energy of your prayers. The asking goes away and you are the expression of the ascension light. Your presence becomes part of the solution to some situation or you reflect this solution to someone else. You anchor the divine completely within you and you are rebirthed into perfection from the baptism that occurs in this sacred Union. The path of ascension takes you from seeking and asking to Union, rebirth, and the full realization of heaven unfolding from within. You feel your oneness with all beings on this planet, with your I AM Presence and with the hierarchy of all Ascended beings. You experience and know everyone's essence as this ascending flame.

The ripple effect

When you embody either the energy of divine Union or any level of the ascension energy, a ripple effect of this sacred energy touches all life on the planet. As a rock thrown into the waters sends out waves that spread out to the shoreline, your energy will move through the world creating ripples that spark the realization of truth and light for others. The sacredness of your energy will plant and ground energy into areas that need healing. The ripple effect will impact committees, communities, governments, and nations. All the sacredness that you embody will reflect onto others. The extent of the capacity of this light is immeasurable. As we come together in groups of Lightworkers and World Servers in sacred Union in the many ways that we do, the collective impact that we have on the ascension of humanity and our planet elevates a thousand times or more. Our shared intention and love for humanity and the earth bring forth peaceful solutions to resolve the world's issues.

Let your beaming light continue to be a catalyst for the transformation and ascension for all humanity and our beautiful planet. Take in the prayers and words of inspiration on the pages that follow as well as any of Danna Fauld's poems in this book. Work with them to assist you in embodying the ascension light, feeding the flame within you.

The journey of ascension does not end here. It is just the beginning. There is no place like home. Welcome home to your ascended nature!

Creator,

Walk with me down this road I call life.

Shine your Light so that I can see a new reality.

Help me to release and heal those false beliefs that keep me from fully experiencing Your Light.

Open my heart. Open my eyes. Open my mind to know the wonders and joys of all Creation.

Let my Spirit sing and dance in celebration of knowing my Oneness with all life on this planet.

Amen

I AM

I AM an endless source of joy and love

I am the knowing that comes from my I AM Presence

I AM an eternal light

I am extending harmony and peace into the world

I AM that I AM and so it is, Beloved I AM.

Legions of Light and all Ascended Beings,

Hold me so close that all that I can see is Light

Assist me in integrating this ascension energy

Infuse me with love so that I can remember I AM love

Guide me to the full realization of my I AM nature

Establish within me a response of love, honor and compassion for all life.

Amen

About Dawn Fleming

Dawn Fleming is an author, lecturer, healer, channeler, and teacher. She is here to assist humanity to make great leaps in transformation as she considers herself to be an energy healer and a catalyst for change. Dawn teaches many energy related workshops as well as classes on alchemy and ascension. She is the Director of Energy Transformations and Infinite Wisdom Press. Dawn works with energy, sacred geometry and various energy tools to create transformation. Through her writing, teaching, and prayer activity, she is assisting humanity's and our planet's ascension.

Dawn is the author of *Creating a Successful Holistic Health Practice*, *Navigating the CEU Process*, *Passing on Wisdom: Keys to Teaching Holistic Health and Spiritual Workshops*, *and Shared*

Wisdom as well as a Reiki I and II manual set published in both English and Spanish. She has recorded several meditation CDs that assist people in their healing, transformation, and ascension processes to include: *Journey into the Heart of the Beloved, Transformed by Prayer, Tranquil Meditations,* and *Healing with Meditation and Prayer.*

Dawn is married, and lives in Arizona with her husband Bill. She enjoys hiking, kayaking, being in nature, and travelling. She has two lovely daughters who are busy spreading their light onto the planet.

Join her email list and receive a free e-zine once every other month. By signing up you will receive the e-book *Shared Wisdom.*

Website: www.energytransformations.org

Email address: reikidawn@yahoo.com

Books and CDs can be ordered at:
www.energytransformations.org/products.html.

Bibliography and Footnotes

Chapter 1

Bibliography

Alder, Vera Stanley. *Finding the Third Eye.* New York: Weisner, 1973.

Cota-Robles, Patricia. *The Awakening.* Tucson. New Age Study of Humanities Purpose, 1993.

Dannelley, Richard. *Sedona, Beyond the Vortex.* Sedona. Light Technology, 1995.

King, Godfree Ray. *Unveiled Mysteries.* Mt. Shasta: Ascended Masters Teaching Foundation, 1986.

King, Godfree Ray. *The Magic Presence.* Schaumburg: Saint Germain Press, 1992.

Melchizedek, Drunvalo. *The Ancient Secret of the Flower of Life.* 2 Volumes. Sedona: Light Technology, 2003.

Melchizedek, Drunvalo. *Living in the Heart.* Sedona: Light Technology, 2003.

Papastavro, Tellis. *Gnosis and the Law.* Tucson: Bulkow, 1972.

Sugru, Thomas. *There is a River. Story of Edgar Cayce.* New York: Weisner, 1959.

Chapter 4

Footnotes

[1] Deepak Chopra, M.D., *Perfect Health, The Complete Mind/Body Guide* (Harmony Books, 1993), p. 7.

[2] http://www. Flouridealert.org/pesticidesodium.f.pineal.htm

Chapter 5

Bibliography

A Course in Miracles. New York: Penguin Books, 1996

Chapter 6

Footnotes

[1] Dr. Ernst Hartmann, "Krankheit als Standortproblem", Haug Verlag, Heidelberg, 5.Auflage 1986

[2] Blanche Merz, Points of Cosmic Energy, Daniel, 1987

[3] Freiherr Gustav von Pohl, *Earth Currents as Pathogenic Agents for Illness and the Development of Cancer*, Frieich Verlag, Feucht, 1983

[4] Christopher Bird, *The Divining Hand*, (Dutton, 1979)

[5] Dr. Harmut Muller and Dipl. Ing Eduard Krausz, *Fundamentals of Global Scaling, A New Physics*, (Raum & Zeit, Special 1, 2002, Germany)

[6] Dr. John A. Wheeler and Ignazio Ciufolini, *Gravitation and Inertia,* (Princeton Press, 1995)

[7] Dr. Walter Russell, *Secret of Light*, (University of Science and Philosophy, 1947)

[8] Dr. William A. Tiller, *Toward a Quantitative Model of Local and*

Non-Local Energetic/Information Healing and Psychoenergetic Science, (Pavior Press, 2007)

[9] The harmonizer device that the Gmac box is attached to is a Life Light ™ tool developed by Slim Spurling for numerous uses.

[10] Dr. Robert J Gilbert, Sacred Geometry Foundation Training, Vesica, 2004, Asheville, NC

[11] Thomas Bearden Phd, *Energy from the Vacuum*, (Cheniere Press, 2002)

[12] Laurent Meijer, Armelle Jezequel, Progress in Cell Cycle Research Vol 4, Springer 2000. Research into biological cell cycles indicates that cells may use a 12 minute cycle to "inhale" nutrients and "exhale" nucleic waste.

Chapter 7

Footnotes

[1] Ascension. CatholicRefernce.net http://www.catholicreference.net/index.cfm?id=31985 (Accessed November 5, 2008).

[2] *A Course in Miracles*, Combined Volume, 2nd Edition. (Mill Valley, CA: Foundation for Inner Peace.) T-21.in.1:7

[3] James Redfield, 1995. *The Celestine Prophecy* (New York: Grand Central Publishing, 1995)

[4] Peter H.Brown and Robert S. Rans. *Material Girl*. (EMI Music Publishing, 1985)

[5] Esoteric Teachings / God Thoughts. #6 - Everything Is Important And Nothing Is Important. http://www.goddirect.org/teach/esotch6.htm (accessed January 8, 2008)

⁶ The Sacred Art of Grounding. http://www.powersthatbe.com/mystic_now/power_tools/ground_intro.htm. (Accessed January 6, 2008)

⁷ Catherine Ponder, *The Dynamic Laws of Prosperity*. 2 Rev Edition. (Marina del Rey, C: Devoss & Company)

⁸ Louise L. Hay. *Heal Your Body*. Carlsbad, CA: Hay House, Inc.,1988)

⁹ Dan Millman, *The Laws of Spirit: A Tale of Transformation*. (Tiburon, CA: HJ Kramer/New World Library, 1995)

Chapter 8

Footnotes

¹ Hazrat Inayat Khan, *The Complete Sayings of Hazrat Inayat Khan*, (Sufi Order Publications, 1978)

² Hazrat Inayat Khan, *The Complete Sayings of Hazrat Inayat Khan*, (Sufi Order Publications, 1978)

³ Hazrat Inayat Khan , *The Sufi Message of Spiritual Liberty*, (International Headquarters, Sufi Movement, Geneva, 1979)

Chapter 10

Footnotes

¹ *Alcoholics Anonymous. Fourth Edition* (New York:Alcoholics Anonymous World Services, Inc., 2001), p. xiii.

² Ibid., p. 63.

³ Ibid., p.76.

About Energy Transformations
Infinite Wisdom Press
Egyptian Healing Rods

Energy Transformations was incorporated in 2004 by Dawn Fleming to provide quality services, learning experiences/workshops, retreats and products that support spiritual growth, transformation, healing and ascension. Energy Transformations is about developing clients and students to reach their full potential as they embrace the ascension journey.

Infinite Wisdom Press, established as a division of Energy Transformations in 2007, uses the power of the written and spoken word to serve the planet in healing the illusions and to restore Oneness, Love, and the Divine Plan. Infinite Wisdom Press publishes books relating to the various aspects of holistic health, energywork, spirituality, and ascension and produces a variety of meditation CDs to assist people to reduce stress, heal, and deepen their meditation practices. Infinite Wisdom Press also produces a series of meditation CDs to assist the ascension process to include *Journey into the Heart of the Beloved* and *Transformed by Prayer*. The Learning Series is another series of CDs that Infinite Wisdom Press produces to add to

our knowledge in the fields of holistic health, transformation, and ascension. http://www.energytransformations.org/products.html
Email: infinitewisdomnow@gmail.com

Egyptian Healing Rods are tools for transformation, healing, and ascension. They are easy to use and here on this planet to assist us on the journey to wholeness.

To learn more about these amazing tools or to purchase a set go to http://www.energytransformations.org/rods.html or http://www.egyptianrods.com

www.ingramcontent.com/pod-product-compliance
Lightning Source LLC
Chambersburg PA
CBHW020757160426
43192CB00006B/351